The Minnesota Model

The Evolution of the Multidisciplinary Approach To Addiction Recovery

Jerry Spicer, M.H.A.

Hazelden Educational Materials
Center City, Minnesota 55012-0176

Library of Congress Cataloging In Publication Data
Spicer, Jerry.
   The Minnesota Model: The evolution of the multidisciplinary
approach to addiction recovery / Jerry Spicer.
      p. cm.
   Includes bibliographical references and index.
   ISBN 0-89486-846-2
   1. Substance abuse—Treatment. 2. Substance abuse—Treatment—
Minnesota—History. I. Title.
RC564.S7 1993
362.29'18'09776—dc20   92-44556
                                                          CIP

Editor's note
Hazelden Educational Materials offers a variety of information on
chemical dependency and related areas. Our publications do not
necessarily represent Hazelden's programs, nor do they officially speak
for any Twelve Step organization.

Manuscript Editor: Debora O'Donnell-Tavolier
Acquisitions Editor: Bill Chickering
Cover design: Theresa Jaeger
Copywriter: Sandra Haus
Typesetter: Northwestern Printcrafters
Proofreader: Caryn Pernu
Production Editor: Cynthia Madsen
Print Manager: Joan Seim
Printer: Bang Printing
The typeface used in this book is Goudy.

To the pioneers and reformers who taught us new ways
to help others and thereby made each of us a better person;
and to the future generations of leaders who must continue
to carry the message.

Contents

Contents

Preface

In 1978 I arrived at Hazelden's campus in Center City, Minnesota, to interview for a position as manager of the research and quality assurance department. I was struck by the beauty of the grounds, the kindness of the staff, and the scale and diversity of Hazelden's mission.

I came to Hazelden from a job in Canada, where government funding was the way people got help. And I was familiar with debates in the research community about controlled drinking—a topic that challenges some basic assumptions of the Minnesota Model. As the day progressed, my concerns gave way to excitement about Hazelden and the Minnesota Model. That's an excitement that I still have in 1993 as president of Hazelden.

I remember my first impressions of Hazelden. The building and grounds gave evidence that here was a place where respect and dignity were "in the bricks"—no locked buildings, no staff wearing white coats to separate themselves from the patients, no people kept in pajamas to reinforce their identity as passive, sick patients. The staff were practical, experienced professionals from all disciplines, who worked as a team to address the complex needs of their clients. They carefully balanced some cynicism about researchers like me with a willingness to go on record with the outcomes of the Minnesota Model they so strongly supported.

Hazelden's commitment to outcome, too, was unique—the belief that human beings, even those struggling with addictions, can change and grow; and the related emphasis on relationships, mutual help, quality of life, and spirituality. Taken as a whole, Hazelden added up to far more than what I'd been taught to research—ounces of ethanol consumed per day!

Hazelden must have liked something about me, too, because I got the job and continued to have many wonderful opportunities. Only after working here for a while did I begin to truly understand some vital parts of the Minnesota Model—the power of the self-help movement and the transformation people and families can experience.

Transformation is the only word I can think of to describe what happens to individuals and families when the Minnesota Model works. They don't define themselves in terms of the addiction anymore; instead, they use words like *recovering* to describe the new directions their lives are taking. Notice that I used the word *recovering*, not *recovered*. Implicit in this choice of words is the idea that recovery is a process that takes place one day at a time over the course of a lifetime.

But there is much more to the Minnesota Model than its practical and theoretical sides. The Model is also a social reform movement of major import. The pioneers of this model redefined alcoholism (and later drug addiction) as *chemical dependency*—not sin or moral weakness. They taught us that alcoholics and addicts do not belong in locked mental wards, and that treating chemically dependent people with dignity and respect in a caring environment can accomplish what few thought possible. These pioneers also taught us the value of involving professionals from many disciplines in treating chemical dependency. But most important, they taught us that a philosophy of long-term rehabilitation offers more than the search for an elusive "cure."

As a movement of social reform, the model and the movement are not yet complete. Prejudices and stereotypes about alcoholics and addicts continue to resurface and erode public support for the person with chemical dependency. The result is that chemical dependency programs must fight harder and harder for the shrinking health care dollar.

We must continue to advocate for these programs. In the language of Alcoholics Anonymous, we must continue to "carry the message" of recovery to policymakers at all levels. As treatment providers, we must continue to hone our knowledge and skills, and to separate tradition from values. (No one, for example, claims that the Minnesota Model is accessible only in freestanding treatment centers that offer a twenty-eight day residential program.) And last, we do well to remember that this whole enterprise rests, as it always has, on one person helping another.

When I first began thinking about a book on the Minnesota Model, I soon realized how big the subject truly is. The model combines psychological theory with a belief in the importance of the human spirit. It is applied in a variety of settings to people with alcohol, drug, and other addiction problems. Started nearly a half-century ago with roots in the program of Alcoholics Anonymous, the model continues to expand throughout the world, broadening its impact to other cultures and buoyed by the remarkable growth of the self-help movement.

Putting this book together required the contributions of many people. I am grateful to those who shared their perspectives during research conducted for this book. The perspective on the Minnesota Model presented here is only one; other supporters of the model may disagree with me on certain points. In a way, however, this testifies to the power of the model—it is a body of ideas that acknowledges disagreement and the need for change and growth. Anyone's perspective on the model is only a snapshot in time, one that reflects our current beliefs about a dynamic process.

Though this book acknowledges criticisms not only of the Minnesota Model but of the recovery movement in general, my primary purpose is not to apologize for or defend the model, but to explain it and set it in a historical context. From that vantage point, we can see what may be the prime contribution of the model—restoring dignity and respect to the treatment of people who live with chemical dependency. History has not always been kind to these people, and even today we find those who assert that alcoholics and addicts should be jailed, censured, or simply ignored. The fact that we now have a well-articulated alternative to these views is the greatest legacy of the Minnesota Model.

In a real sense, there is not a Minnesota Model but many Minnesota Models, all shaded by the views of individuals and shaped by the messy, day-to-day realities of helping people find an alternative to using alcohol or other drugs. Some in the federal government will argue that too little data exist on the model's effectiveness, and even a casual observation of treatment programs yields extreme variations in the application and practice of the model.

Perhaps the most reasonable position is to consider the Minnesota Model as an ideal—one that is desired and never completely achieved. This is understandable, given that the model is a complex mixture of values, assumptions, clinical practices, people, and communities. Included is that rainbow of self-help groups that take as their core the Twelve Steps of Alcoholics Anonymous.

Whatever form it takes, the Minnesota Model is probably the leading method for treating alcohol and other drug abuse. Put simply, most people who today receive treatment for these conditions will experience the influence of this model firsthand. It is therefore crucial for us to take a second look at the model and make certain that we truly understand it.

Acknowledgments

I would like to thank Doug Toft for his great help and skill in crafting the language and ideas for this book. His assistance was invaluable in bringing my ideas and those of all the people intereviewed into a clearer focus. Throughout the project his enthusiasm and commitment to the importance of what we were saying never flagged.

A Tale of Recovery

Suppose for a moment that it is 1940. If you are an alcoholic, your addiction will probably be met with one of these responses:

- You will be committed to a locked ward in a hospital, which you will share with mental patients.
- You will be jailed or imprisoned.
- Your addiction will be denied and ignored.

Back in 1940, options for alcoholics in the United States consisted largely of beds for "inebriates" in hospitals that provided little or no treatment. Research on alcoholism was scant. Alcoholics Anonymous was just getting started, and the medical and psychiatric establishments had publicly declared it useless.

Fast-forward to 1993. Today, in the United States alone, there are over seven thousand treatment programs and centers for alcoholism, drug abuse, and other addictions. There are outpatient and inpatient programs, aftercare programs, halfway houses, family programs, community education and outreach programs, and other forms of treatment, education, and support.

According to at least one estimate, as many as 95 percent of all these programs are based—strictly or loosely—on a single model for treatment and recovery. This model began during the late 1940s and early 1950s at three centers in the state of Minnesota. Today it is known as the *Minnesota Model*.

Introduction

How did we change from a nation that neglected and jailed people with addictions to one with the most extensive and effective network of recovery programs in the world?

Thereby hangs a tale.

The Minnesota Model tells this tale. At the center of the story is the model itself: a comprehensive, multidisciplinary treatment program emphasizing caring instead of curing, one that focuses on the spiritual growth and dignity of the individual.

The Minnesota Model is considered by many observers to be the foremost and most effective form of chemical dependency treatment in the United States today. Interest in the Minnesota Model among chemical dependency counselors and other recovery professionals continues to grow. And over the years it has been improved and refined. Recently it has been adapted for use in Europe, South America, and elsewhere. Yet there currently exists no detailed or up-to-date account of the Minnesota Model.

I hope this book fills that gap. Its aim is to offer an overview and history of the Minnesota Model. In addition, this book will consider some of the criticisms aimed at the model and look at how it may be changed and applied in the future. While *The Minnesota Model* is intended to be of direct use to chemical dependency counselors and other recovery professionals, it is also meant to appeal to a broad readership. I hope the book will appeal to anyone with an interest in recovery.

This book will look at the model from eight angles. Chapter 1, "Before the Minnesota Model," urges us to understand its historical significance. It reviews the role intoxicants have played in human life and how our culture has responded to people with drinking problems.

Alcohol and other drugs have been an integral part of culture and civilization since ancient times. One prominent example is colonial America, where heavy drinking was the social norm. Reactions to that norm led to the rise of temperance movements and, ultimately, to Prohibition. Since the repeal of Prohibition, Americans have had a love-hate relationship with mind-altering chemicals. This attitude undermines an effective public response to the chemically dependent person. Soon after Prohibition came another social experiment that paved the way for the Minnesota Model: Alcoholics Anonymous. This chapter offers a brief summary of AA's beginning and its core principles.

Chapter 2, "The Minnesota Model Is Born," tells the story of three treatment programs that served as laboratories in developing the Minnesota Model. The first was Pioneer House, started by a recovering alcoholic named Patrick Cronin in 1948. In 1949 came Hazelden, a "guest house for alcoholics of the professional class," formed by a group of businessmen. At first, Hazelden's program was based largely on AA. As the organization expanded, however, its treatment program incorporated the tools of modern clinical psychology and medical treatment—two crucial components of the Minnesota Model.

Then in 1950, a team of professionals led by Nelson Bradley introduced several innovations in alcoholism treatment at a third Minnesota program: Willmar State Hospital. Bradley had the audacity to unlock the doors of the treatment wards, separate alcoholics from mental patients, and hire recovering alcoholics as counselors. Over the next ten years, Willmar merged AA principles with the skills of a multidisciplinary team: psychologists, physicians, and members of the clergy. This practice, too, became part of the Minnesota Model.

As explained in chapter 3, "Understanding the Minnesota Model," there are still many ways to define the model. In fact, it may even be more accurate to speak of Minnesota Models. Reduced to their common denominators, however, nearly all Minnesota models share three beliefs about treatment: (1) treat people with chemical dependency instead of locking them up or ignoring them, (2) treat them with dignity, and (3) help them recover physically, mentally, and spiritually.

Chapter 4, "Progress and Problems—1950 to 1990," talks about the strength of the Minnesota Model on three fronts:

- Treatment centers based on the Minnesota Model gained *therapeutic* force as they grew at an explosive rate and became accredited.
- Treatment gained *political* force as represented by new governmental agencies (such as the NIAAA) and legislation (such as the Hughes Act of 1970).
- Treatment gained *financial* force as insurance carriers began to pay for treatment.

During the latter part of this period, however, some nagging political, economic, and social problems developed: cutbacks in governmental funding that undermined treatment efforts, the growth of managed care companies and cost containment, and a regression to attitudes that stigmatize alcoholics and addicts and those who treat them.

Very few people are neutral when it comes to the Minnesota Model. This is the subject of chapter 5, "Critics and Criticism." Objections to the Minnesota Model fall into three basic categories:

- *Objections to the spiritual basis.* Specifically, critics object to the "Higher Power" orientation of AA.
- *Objections to the "disease concept."* Critics of the model argue that the disease concept is contradictory and applied to so many behaviors that it has become meaningless. Critics also believe the concept ignores the role of personal choice in developing an addiction and sustaining recovery.
- Objections to the basic model assumption that *chemical dependency is best treated as a primary condition.* Critics of the model view alcoholism and other forms of addiction as symptoms of other conditions and thus offer psychiatric and behaviorist models of treatment.

These weaknesses, say the critics, undermine the effectiveness of chemical dependency treatment.

A point-by-point reply to critics of the Minnesota Model is beyond the scope of this book. However, we can eliminate some misunderstanding. That is the focus of chapter 6, "Three Points About the Minnesota Model."

First, the Minnesota Model offers an inclusive, flexible spirituality that is distinct and separate from organized religion. Second, the disease concept is logically defensible and therapeutically useful. The anatomy of alcoholism can be compared with that of other, "legitimate" diseases. The Minnesota Model treats chemical dependency as a disease because this makes sound clinical sense: it advocates humane treatment for addicts, improves access to treatment, and promotes abstinence. Finally, the question of whether chemical dependency should be treated as a primary condition is best answered by evaluating the results of that treatment. Although studies of treatment outcomes pose serious methodological challenges, research does offer support for the effectiveness of the Minnesota Model. Moreover, a new model of research and evaluation—the study of recovery pathways—offers great help and hope for the future.

Chapter 7, "Challenges and Possible Futures," reminds us that practitioners of the Minnesota Model face continuing challenges. Among them are shaping public policy during the next wave of health care reform, responding to the global increase in addiction, meeting the challenge of chronic illness, and much more.

Reflecting on these challenges, we return to a key point of this book: *The Minnesota Model is a collection of perspectives on treatment, not a set of rigid prescriptions.* As such, it is open-ended and pragmatic—qualities that make it well suited to meet future treatment needs.

Remember, too, the importance of the Minnesota Model as a movement of social reform. The model played a major role in transforming treatment wards from "snake pits" into places where alcoholics and addicts could retain their dignity. External elements of the Minnesota Model may change, including the length of stay and methods of reimbursement. Given economic and political forces, they may have to change. But it's hard to see how the core perspectives of the model could be lost, since they are now widely assumed to be the very starting points of treatment. And beyond promoting any specific model is a higher ideal: doing whatever it takes to help people recover, whether or not we call it the Minnesota Model.

The Appendix is an intellectual tour de force—a wide-ranging interview with Daniel J. Anderson, president emeritus of Hazelden and one of the architects of the Minnesota Model. Anderson not only summarizes much of the material from this book but also gives a moving firsthand account of his experiences at Willmar State Hospital in the early 1950s.

The central theme of this book can be stated simply: *The Minnesota Model represents a social reform movement that has humanized the treatment of people addicted to alcohol and other drugs.* Our imperative is to educate people about the pressing need for humane treatment programs. In this sense, the Minnesota Model must be reinvented and reaffirmed for each generation.

The Minnesota Model is the first book to give an up-to-date perspective on the Minnesota Model. It is a story I hope you find useful and enjoyable.

CHAPTER ONE

Before the Minnesota Model

Drinking Alcohol: An Ancient Legacy

For reasons that still aren't clear, human beings have felt a persistent need to tinker with their internal worlds by using mood-altering chemicals. Alcohol, in particular, is bound up with daily life because of its many ceremonial uses.

Indeed, drinking has been an indispensable part of daily social, religious, and political life for several thousand years.[1] Probably the oldest known drink is *mead*, a fermented honey.[2]

The first written records of alcoholic beverages are on clay tablets produced by the ancient Babylonians. These records, dating back to 5,000 B.C., refer to beer. Beer was brewed by priestesses, who believed the drink was a gift from the gods and used it in religious rites. The ancient Egyptians also drank beer. They believed the recipe for brewing this alcohol was a divine secret revealed by the goddess Isis.[3]

Wine dates back to 3,000 B.C., according to records from Mesopotamia.[4] It was a popular drink throughout the ancient world, favored by the Hebrews, Greeks, and Romans. Classical mythology celebrates Dionysus, or Bacchus, the god of wine. He is usually depicted wearing a crown of grapes and clasping a wine goblet. The Greeks worshiped him not only for the gift of wine but for grape harvests and fertility in general. It was among the Romans that the once-solemn celebrations became the orgiastic *bacchanalia*, hence the association of Bacchus with drunkenness and revelry.[5]

The Bible also contains references to alcohol. It tells us that Noah discovered wine, and when he left the ark after the great flood, one of his first acts was to plant a vineyard.

Wine is part of the Seder, the first ritual meal during the Jewish feast of Passover. Wine is also used in a sacrament that traces its origins to Passover. The Bible tells us that Jesus blessed the bread and wine during the last supper with his disciples. He asked them to remember him by repeating this sacred act — the origin of the rite that became known as the Lord's Supper and is still practiced today in many churches.

Alcohol has accompanied other human activities of great scale, including war. Herodotus, a Greek historian of the fifth century B.C., wrote about a war waged by Cyaxares, king of Media and Persia, against the Scythians. During this conflict, Cyaxares waged a "wet" battle, inviting his enemies to a drinking feast. The Scythians got the most intoxicated and succumbed to Cyaxares' forces.[6] Centuries later, George Washington's army would also be big alcohol customers. Included in each soldier's daily provisions was a liquor ration of about four ounces. Alcohol was considered a necessity, given the conditions under which these soldiers fought during the American Revolution. Congress even sent the troops thirty extra casks of whiskey as a consolation for losing the Battle of Germantown in 1777.[7]

Alcohol and political decision making also have a long partnership. The Saxons, who ruled England in the seventh and eighth centuries A.D., drank beer at their councils.[8] And the ancient Greeks staged *symposia*, which were drinking clubs frequented by politicians.

Religious orders kept the secrets of wine making alive during the Middle Ages, safeguarding the drink for use in religious ceremonies. After the fall of the Roman empire, in fact, Christian monks were among the few who knew how to make wine. Champagne, one of the most enduringly popular wines, was first developed by a Benedictine monk, Dom Pierre Pérignon.[9] And Chablis comes to us from Cisterian monks who named the wine after their abbey.[10]

Wine and beer were the favored alcoholic drinks in the Western world during the Middle Ages, and were commonplace at social events. In fact, there was such a high value placed on wine that some fuedal lords used it as currency to pay debts.[11]

Distillation: A Medieval Discovery

Mead, beer, and wine: each of these drinks has one thing in common—a moderate amount of alcohol. That changed in the eighth century A.D., when an Arab named Jabir ibn Hayyan, commonly called Geber, discovered how to distill alcoholic drinks. Boasting skills in fields as diverse as medicine and magic, Geber took part in the alchemist's quest to find the secret formula that would transform metal into gold. His discovery of distillation was an accidental result of his efforts to reach this goal. Through distillation, Geber burned away the impurities that form when wine ferments. The result was a more concentrated liquid, which he called *al kuhul,* or "alcohol."[12]

Distillation was then rediscovered in thirteenth-century France by Arnauld de Villeneuve, a professor at the University of Montpellier. Believing that he had discovered a potent cure for many diseases, de Villeneuve called this new form of alcohol *aqua vitae*— literally, the "water of life."

Distillation was a turning point in our love affair with liquor. Armed with this technology, drinkers could enjoy a purer, more concentrated form of alcohol than ever before. From the fifteenth through the seventeenth centuries, use of distilled drinks spread throughout Europe. This, combined with the tumultuous social and political change taking place during that period, resulted in a dramatic rise in the quantity of alcohol consumed—and its accompanying problems.

Heavy Drinking: Alcohol Consumption in Colonial America

Colonial Americans followed the lead of Europe. Existing records about drinking practices of colonial Americans point us to one con-

clusion: people drank a lot. Today we might call them heavy drinkers; to them, it was the natural course of things. To people who
recalled polluted water supplies in Europe, wine and beer seemed a
safer bet. Add to this another incentive: alcohol kept well at sea,
while water often went bad.

Historians Mark Lender and James Martin estimate that the average colonial American in the late eighteenth century drank a little less than six gallons of absolute alcohol each year. To put this
figure in perspective, that's about thirty-four gallons of beer. This
figure is an *average* for all people over age fifteen at the time—a
group that included nondrinkers. Individual drinkers could have
consumed much more than the thirty-four-gallon average. Compare
this with the figure for Americans in the early 1980s: 2.9 gallons of
beer per person, per year.[13] "Besides," note Lender and Martin,
"the wisdom of the day held that alcohol was essential for good
health: A stiff drink warmed a person on cold nights and kept out
chills and fevers; a few glasses made hard work easier to bear, aided
digestion, and in general helped sustain the constitution."[14]

Distilled beverages were held in such high regard that they were
sometimes used as wages. In the 1640s, the town fathers of Boston
voted to stop this practice. The result was an immediate labor strike,
which brought the new law to an end.[15]

The prevailing colonial ethos was to drink often and to drink a
lot. Even children drank alcohol during family meals—mostly beer
and fermented cider. It was common to serve alcohol to workers at
communal projects, including church construction and land clear-
ing, since consuming alcohol could ease the pain of the backbreak-
ing labor. Weddings, baptisms, and holiday feasts were wet
gatherings. So were ordinations for ministers and even funerals.[16]

Though liquor flowed freely in colonial America, we find only
isolated reports of problem drinkers. There is at least one explanation: even though the colonials loved alcohol, they deplored public
drunkenness. People caught drunk in public faced jail terms, stiff
fines, stocks, and even the lash. Moreover, the ideals of family and

community membership were sacrosanct. All these social sanctions worked to keep drinkers' behavior largely in check.[17]

But as America expanded westward, communities became more scattered and difficult to govern. Ties to family and community loosened, and the liquor flowed more freely.

Benjamin Rush —
Early Advocate of the Disease Concept

In 1784 Dr. Benjamin Rush, a signer of the Declaration of Independence, almost single-handedly launched the temperance movement in America. His weapon was a widely circulated pamphlet titled *An Inquiry into the Effects of Ardent Spirits on the Human Mind and Body.*

Keeping in tune with prevailing views, Rush did not condemn the use of beer and wine. Consumed in moderate quantities, Rush believed, these beverages could promote health. Included in the *Inquiry* was "A Moral and Physical Thermometer"—a chart that listed the popular drinks of the time along with the likely consequences of consuming them. Listed as being consistent with "temperance, health, and wealth" were water, milk, and small beer, which Rush associated with "Serenity of Mind, Reputation, Long Life, & Happiness." Wine and strong beer were likewise associated with "Cheerfulness, Strength, and Nourishment, when taken only in small quantities, and at meals."[18]

He was not nearly so kind to "ardent spirits," or distilled liquor. Rush's chart linked distilled drinks with vices, diseases, and appropriate punishments. For example, punch had as its vices idleness and gaming, sickness, and debt; toddy and egg rum were associated with "peevishness," "tremors of the hands in the morning," "puking," and the threat of jail.[19] In fairness to Rush, he did not assert that such links were hard-and-fast. His point was only to convince a wide audience that alcohol addiction was a progressive condition with debilitating consequences.

In addition to sounding a call for abstinence from distilled drinks, Rush was the first American writer to pronounce chronic drunkenness a disease. He viewed this disease as progressive and marked by identifiable stages. According to Rush, alcohol was also an addictive agent, and the addict's ability to control drinking was clearly impaired. In these respects, Rush's writing on the disease concept of alcoholism was strikingly modern.

THE TEMPERANCE MOVEMENT LEADS TO PROHIBITION

Early temperance groups in America took their cue from Rush, calling not for total abstinence but moderation in drinking. But what is now called the classic temperance movement, which lasted over a century (from 1830 to about 1940), took a markedly different stance: any use of beverage alcohol was an evil to be vigorously opposed; total abstinence was the only sane course.

This message worked. By 1835 the American Temperance Society estimated that two million people had quit drinking distilled liquor and that four thousand distilleries had closed since the beginning of the movement. Per capita consumption of alcohol peaked at about seven gallons of absolute alcohol per year in 1830. By 1840, that figure had dropped to about three gallons. As far as we know, this is the largest drop in alcohol consumption during any decade in American history.[20]

The 1840s saw the rise of the Washingtonian Temperance Society, a group founded by drinkers to help other drinkers. The founders were six men previously unconnected with any temperance group. One night in 1840, these men met at Chase's Tavern in Baltimore. Tradition has it that their conversation drifted to the subject of the effect that drinking had on their lives. One of those present then agreed to attend a nearby temperance lecture. Immediately after the lecture, this man "took the pledge"—that is, vowed to stop drinking. He and his friends from Chase's Tavern agreed to work individually with other drinkers who wished to stop drinking.

12

The Washingtonians' sole aim was to help individual drinkers take the pledge. As such, they were not a large-scale social reform movement. Even with their commitment to work on a smaller scale, however, they made an impact: about 600,000 people took the pledge through the efforts of this group; perhaps 150,000 of these actually remained abstinent.[21]

By 1850, the Washingtonians were in decline. They lacked a central organization or coherent program. Other temperance groups took the group's fate as evidence for strong social reform: the battle against "ardent spirits" could be won only through legislation, not through the private efforts of drinkers seeking to help each other.

The Women's Christian Temperance Union (WCTU) was formed in 1874, and took the nation one step closer to Prohibition. The group's original tactic was to hold "pray-ins" at saloons, asking the owners to close their drinking establishments. Later the group knelt in front of hotels, pharmacies, and other places that sold liquor.

Working with other temperance groups, the WCTU helped to launch Reform Clubs, self-governed groups that resembled the Alcoholics Anonymous of today. And like the Washingtonians, members of Reform Clubs agreed to help one another stay sober.

The impact of all these groups was a shift in the country's norms. An 1848 print by Currier and Ives offers a telling example. This print depicted George Washington offering a toast to his officers. Near him, on a table, was a bottle of liquor. In 1876, a new rendering of the same event removed both the glass and the bottle.[22]

Treatment in Nineteenth-Century America

During the late nineteenth and early twentieth centuries, thousands of Americans bet their hopes for sobriety on the "Keeley cure," also known as the "gold cure." Dr. Leslie Keeley claimed it was nothing less than a cure for alcoholism and other drug addictions. Americans bought the claim. The gold cure was so popular that by 1900 there was at least one Keeley Institute in every state.

What was in Keeley's famed medication for drunks? To this day, that remains unknown. Lender and Martin speculate that the concoction was a mixture of gold salt and vegetable compounds.[23]

Referring to it as "bi-chloride of gold," Keeley claimed that the ingredients—whatever they were—could cure addiction. Keeley preferred that his patients receive an intravenous injection of the medication at one of his institutes. However, he also offered oral doses via mail order.

After 1900, when Keeley died, the credibility of his claims for the "gold cure" suffered. This was the result, in part, of reports that graduates of Keeley's program were relapsing in large numbers.

Today's Keeley's claims seem bizarre, and many are amazed that his ideas were taken seriously. But given the widespread ignorance about alcoholism in Keeley's time, we can understand why people desperately turned to a quick fix for alcoholism, which would later be described by *Alcoholics Anonymous* as "cunning, baffling, and powerful."

Anyone who wanted to treat alcoholics in a medical setting had to battle the accepted view that drunkards were moral reprobates who chose their life of dissipation. Even so, there were signs of progress. During the 1870s, Dr. Joseph Turner called for medical treatment of alcoholics, urging each state to create "inebriate asylums."[24] Another group, the American Association for the Study of Inebriety, took the same stand. The goal of this group was to conduct research on alcohol and drug addiction and establish addiction treatment as a medical specialty. Like Alcoholics Anonymous, the association acknowledged the importance of spirituality in recovery from alcoholism. It differed from AA, however, in that it endorsed Prohibition. AA, as a matter of tradition, has no stand on any outside issues.

The association's efforts led some of its members to establish "asylums," where people addicted to alcohol and other drugs were treated with dignity, sometimes in settings that resembled elegant hotels. Such asylums were the forerunners of treatment centers today.

The Short History of Prohibition—
And the Surviving Stigma

Late in the nineteenth century, the Anti-Saloon League, a well-funded and well-organized temperance group, gained political clout. This organization had the ability to swing votes to any candidate who supported Prohibition. By 1916, many of these candidates had won elections and created unstoppable political momentum for Prohibition.

January 16, 1920, was the crowning day for the temperance movement in America. On that date, the states ratified the Eighteenth Amendment to the U.S. Constitution, and Prohibition became the nation's official policy. As a result 1,077 saloons, 1,247 breweries, and 507 distilleries in the United States were suddenly illegal.[25]

The victory didn't last long. By 1933, the nation's patience with Prohibition ran out. That year the Twenty-First Amendment to the constitution was ratified, which repealed the Eighteenth Amendment. On the day the new law took effect, New York City sent all its police officers to Times Square to deal with the anticipated celebration.[26]

America was officially "wet" again. Or, more accurately, it was "damp": states and counties had the option to remain "dry," and some chose to do so. Even today there is considerable variation in laws across the country regarding who is permitted to drink alcohol, at what age, and under what conditions.

According to Lender and Martin, the collapse of Prohibition ushered in an era that is still with us—the age of "ambivalence."[27] This ambivalence leaves crucial questions unanswered: What constitutes acceptable drinking behavior? What do we teach our children about the use of alcohol and other drugs? And how does a humane society respond to people who become alcoholics or drug addicts? Even in 1993 Americans still lack coherent and widely accepted answers to these questions.

One consequence of this confused attitude was that Americans virtually ignored the problem of treating alcoholics for twenty years after Prohibition was repealed. Attention instead was focused on other issues, including the Great Depression and World War II. Chronic drunkards were usually arrested and jailed with little hope of receiving medical attention. Others were consigned to state hospitals, sharing wards with the mentally ill.

BILL W.'s "HOT FLASH"

Keeping in mind the prevailing view of drunkenness as moral weakness, we can appreciate the courage of Bill W. and Dr. Bob, who informally founded Alcoholics Anonymous in 1935. The group's basic text, *Alcoholics Anonymous*, echoed Rush's idea that alcoholics simply could not control their drinking through sheer, unaided willpower:

> *The fact is that most alcoholics, for reasons yet obscure, have lost the power of choice in drink. Our so-called will power becomes practically nonexistent. We are unable, at certain times, to bring into our consciousness with sufficient force the memory of the suffering and humiliation of even a week or a month ago. We are without defense against the first drink.* [28]

Bill Wilson, co-founder of Alcoholics Anonymous, was an alcoholic stockbroker. Desperate for a way to stay sober, he became involved with the Oxford Group, a nondenominational religious movement seeking to reclaim the spirit of first-century Christianity. Bill was struck by the group's working principles, which called for taking moral inventories and making amends to people harmed by our actions.

Later Bill W. broke with the Oxford Group because it referred to some of its principles as "absolutes." Alcoholics, Bill reasoned, are already absolutists and perfectionists, experts in rigid, all-or-nothing thinking. He also talked about the dangers of "going broke on this sort of perfection—trying to get too good by Thursday."[29] Even so, the Oxford program was a great influence on Bill, and several of its principles found their way into the Twelve Steps of AA.

Despite working with the Oxford Group, Bill continued to drink. One day in 1934, after downing four beers, he checked himself into Towns Hospital in New York City for detoxification. During that stay, Bill finally quit scheming his way to sobriety. In short, he "hit bottom." This is how he described the event years later:

> My depression deepened unbearably and finally it seemed to me as though I were at the bottom of the pit. . . . All at once I found myself crying out, "If there is a God, let Him show Himself! I am ready to do anything, anything!"
>
> Suddenly the room lit up with a great white light. I was caught up into an ecstasy which there are no words to describe. It seemed to me, in the mind's eye, that I was on a mountain and that a wind not of air but of spirit was blowing. And then it burst upon me that I was a free man.[30]

After this experience, affectionately recalled by AA members as Bill's "hot flash," Bill never took another drink.

BILL MEETS DR. BOB:
THE FOUNDING OF ALCOHOLICS ANONYMOUS

By May 1935, Bill was actively working with alcoholics. Desiring to return to work as a stockbroker, he pursued contacts on Wall Street. A business trip took him to Ohio, where he found himself in the lobby of the Mayflower Hotel in Akron on May 11, 1935, nursing the wounds of a failed business deal. At one end of the lobby was the bar swelling with Saturday afternoon patrons; at the other end was a church directory. His first impulse was to get drunk. Panic at that thought convinced him that he needed to talk to another alcoholic. He walked to the directory instead.

There Bill found the name of the Reverend Dr. Walter Tunks, an Episcopalian minister. Bill called the minister, told him his story, and asked for the names of any Oxford Group members in Akron. Tunks gave Bill a list of ten names.

After a series of calls, Bill reached a woman named Henrietta Seiberling. She was a devoted Oxford Group member who had spent the last two years trying to sober up an alcoholic surgeon, Dr. Bob Smith. Sensing Bill's sincerity, Henrietta agreed to introduce Bill to Bob at her house.

Bob had come to Henrietta's on the condition that he and his wife Anne stay no longer than fifteen minutes. Instead, he found himself transfixed by Bill's story. He realized that Bill was a fellow alcoholic and knew firsthand the things that only another alcoholic could know: the shame, the secrets, the firm resolve to quit, and the intellectual gymnastics that led to taking yet another drink.

Bill's conversation with Bob was the first "Twelve Step call": there were no prescriptions for how to quit drinking or preaching about the evils of booze. Bill simply told his story—what happened when he drank, what happened to him at Towns Hospital, and how he managed to stay sober by working with other alcoholics. In his history of Alcoholics Anonymous, Ernest Kurtz notes that Bill ended his narrative with these words, spoken as he rose to leave: "I called Henrietta because I needed another alcoholic. I needed you, Bob, probably a lot more than you'll ever need me. So, thanks a lot for hearing me out. I know now that I'm not going to take a drink, and I'm grateful to you."[31]

For the next three weeks, Bill lived with the Smiths. Their time was structured by the practices of the Oxford Group, including meetings, prayer, and devotional reading. During that time, Bob managed to do something he'd not been able to do in years—stay sober.

Soon Bob decided to attend a medical convention in Atlantic City, New Jersey. His wife feared that Bob's separation from Bill would lead Bob into another drinking spree. Even so, she agreed to her husband's plan. Shortly after the convention, Bob returned to Akron at 4 A.M. one morning, drunk.

Bob was scheduled to perform an operation three days later. During that time, Bill W. and Anne Smith "worked" on Bob, helping him through the withdrawal symptoms and talking to him about Oxford Group principles. On the day of the scheduled surgery, Bill drove Bob to the hospital and handed him a bottle of beer to ward off the shakes during the operation.

The operation was a success. Bob returned home, ready to earnestly apply the principles he'd been absorbing for the past two years. He began by making amends to those he'd harmed through his drinking, including creditors. This time, his sobriety stuck. The day was June 10, 1935, now remembered as Dr. Bob's dry date and the official beginning of AA. The new group's program took definitive shape when it appeared in *Alcoholics Anonymous* (also known as the "Big Book") in 1939.

JUNG AND JAMES SPARK AA SPIRITUALITY

In 1961 Bill W. wrote a letter to Carl Jung, a thank-you for the psychiatrist's influence on the development of Alcoholic's Anonymous. Jung had worked with an alcoholic named Rowland H. in 1931, telling Rowland that his alcoholic condition was nearly hopeless. According to Jung, Rowland's only chance for sobriety was to "become the subject of a spiritual or religious experience—in short, a genuine conversion." Jung also mentioned that such experiences were rare but had been happening to alcoholics for centuries. [32]

Jung responded immediately to Bill's note, writing that Rowland's craving for alcohol was "the equivalent, on a low level, of the spiritual thirst of our being for wholeness, expressed in medieval language: the union with God." The letter ended with these words: "You see, alcohol in Latin is *spiritus* and you use the same word for the highest religious experience as well as for the most depraving poison. The helpful formula therefore is: *spiritus contra spiritum.*"[33]

Bill found the same idea expressed in the writings of philosopher-psychologist William James. Bill regarded James as one of the honorary founders of AA and devoured James's book *The Varieties of*

Religious Experience. Bill's enthusiasm must have been generated by passages such as this one:

> The sway of alcohol over mankind is unquestionably due to its powers to stimulate the mystical faculties of human nature, usually crushed to the earth by the cold facts and dry criticisms of the sober hour. Sobriety diminishes, expands, unites, and says yes. It is in fact the great exciter of the Yes function in man. . . . The drunken consciousness is one bit of the mystic consciousness, and our total opinion of it must find its place in our opinion of that larger whole.[34]

Following these words is a passage in which James reports his personal experience of intoxication from nitrous oxide. His experience convinced him that normal waking consciousness is but one of the many levels of consciousness available to human beings. He called upon his readers to avoid a "premature closing of our accounts with reality," stating that no psychology could safely ignore altered states of consciousness.[35]

One of those altered states was the experience of conversion—the radical shift in thought and feeling that Jung held out as the only hope for Rowland. In *The Varieties of Religious Experience,* James describes in detail conversion experiences dating back to biblical times. Reading James must have been a great comfort to Bill W.—a scholarly assurance that his "hot flash" was not lunacy but a path to restored sanity.

AA's Inclusive View of Spirituality

According to the Big Book, recovery from alcoholism rests on the kinds of experiences that Jung and James described. And though such experiences elude our understanding, they have a profound and obvious effect on alcoholics: an end to drinking.

Bill's account of his sudden spiritual experience remains crucial to the message of the Big Book. After the book's first printing, however, some of its readers feared that they might never have the spectacular conversion that Bill had. Responding to their concerns, Bill added an Appendix to the book. Among AA members, he wrote, dramatic conversions were not the rule by any means. Bill added: "Most of our experiences are what the psychologist William James calls the 'educational variety' because they develop slowly over a period of time."[36]

In this passage, Bill drew a distinction between a *spiritual experience* and a *spiritual awakening*. Spiritual awakenings, though just as far-reaching in their effects, take place gradually through the daily practice of the Twelve Steps. Moreover, any alcoholics who honestly face their problems can recover, provided they remain open to spiritual concepts.

From the beginning, AA has welcomed people who are not religious in any conventional sense, including atheists and agnostics.[37] All that is required for someone to begin the Twelve Step program is a willingness to change. The Big Book puts it this way:

> We needed to ask ourselves but one short question. "Do I now believe, or am I even willing to believe, that there is a power greater than myself?" As soon as a man can say that he does believe, or is willing to believe, we emphatically assure him that he is on his way.[38]

About AA:
Individual Autonomy and "Joyous Pluralism"

Though AA has existed since 1935, it is still widely misunderstood today.

The heart of AA is the idea of mutual help, the idea that people who are part of the problem can be part of the solution. On a daily basis AA members relive Bill's discovery that alcoholics can help each other stay sober.

In his book *Not-God: A History of Alcoholics Anonymous*, Kurtz sums up the core dynamic of AA in a complex but beautiful phrase:

"the shared honesty of mutual vulnerability openly acknowledged."[39] In an AA meeting, members openly share their stories (or, as AA says, "our experience, strength, and hope"), much as Bill shared his with Bob in 1935. By freely admitting the consequences of their addiction, members discover the strength to stay sober one day at a time.

AA is concerned primarily with the *alcoholic* more than *alcoholism*. Its purpose is to help people achieve sobriety on a day-to-day basis — not to conduct controlled research on alcoholism or promote a comprehensive theory of alcoholism. To the question "What is alcoholism?" an AA pamphlet offers this simple response:

> The explanation that seems to make sense to most A.A. members is that alcoholism is an illness, a *progressive* illness, which can never be cured but which, like some other diseases, can be arrested. Going one step further, many A.A.s feel that the illness represents the combination of a physical sensitivity to alcohol and a mental obsession with drinking, which, regardless of consequences, cannot be broken by willpower alone.[40]

Like all meetings based on the Twelve Steps, AA meetings are free. Moreover, people who attend are free to leave the group at any time. The only requirement for joining AA is a "desire to stop drinking" — period. There is no central body in AA with binding authority to enforce its will on local groups. AA does, however, maintain a central office (AA World Services in New York City) that advises local groups, publishes literature, answers requests, and maintains contact with the press, radio, and television.

AA is not a temperance movement — one that suggests the public give up drinking liquor in any form. In fact, the organization acknowledges that drinking can be a source of constructive pleasure for many people. Members of AA simply acknowledge that they personally cannot "handle the stuff."

Moreover, AA does not claim to be the only path to sobriety.

When asked about other methods of treatment, one AA member said, "I'm for anything that helps alcoholics recover!"[41] This statement is a perfect summary of the spirit of AA.

UNDERSTANDING THE TWELVE STEPS

What animates the Steps are some simple, timeless principles. Daniel J. Anderson, president emeritus of the Hazelden Foundation and an architect of the Minnesota Model, offers this colorful summary of those principles:[42]

1. *Get Honest:* All of us—recovering and nonrecovering people alike—can benefit from this principle. It's a universal human tendency to deny what's unpleasant, to close our eyes to the brute facts. We rationalize away our weaknesses. We exaggerate our strengths.

2. *Get With People:* If we want to make long-term changes in our behavior, then we're called on to band with other people whose mission is to make a similar change. Together, we can teach each other. Our very admission of weakness and the need for mutual help can transform out limitations into strengths.

3. *Turn to God/Higher Power:* Believing in God or a Higher Power is not a prerequisite for taking this step. All that's required is a quality referred to in the Steps as *willingness.* The irony is that for all their references to spirituality, the Steps are reasonable, empirical—even hard-nosed. They take the form of of an ongoing experiment. Nothing in the Steps need be taken on faith. Rather, each of us is encouraged to verify their efficacy for ourselves. This humble beginning is enough to initiate a lasting change.

4. *Clean House—But Get Advice First on How to Do It:* If we wish to be free of the mental habits that promote drinking and drugging, we need to tell the truth, and tell that truth to others. We must tell them what we have been and what we have

done. Beyond that, we must restore what has been stolen, repair what has been damaged, and work with others to put things right. The Twelve Step tradition has evolved a number of guidelines for doing this—suggestions for making amends in a way that does not cause further harm to others.

5. *Get in Shape:* As recovering people we are flabby and out of shape in a myriad of ways—not only physically, but emotionally, socially, and spiritually. To get back in shape, we can cultivate daily "exercises": practices such as bibliotherapy that remold our thinking, and daily meditation and prayer.

6. *Help Your Brother/Sister:* For a person well on the path of recovery, giving and receiving become linked. Initially, however, we might feel so weak that we have little to give others. At this stage, it is all right to take; later, we will be in a position to give. Help has been freely given us to us; the most fitting response is to give freely in return. Here is one of the great paradoxes of the spiritual path: To keep the program, we must give it away.

SOME LESSONS OF HISTORY

America's response to mind-altering chemicals and those who use them comes in cycles—moral condemnation of alcoholics and addicts, followed by enlightened calls for more humane treatment; attempts to interdict the supplies of chemicals, followed by efforts at prevention and education to moderate the demand.

The checkered history of our response flows directly from our deep-seated ambivalence. And that ambivalence, in turn, makes it difficult to shape any coherent public policy response to the problem of addiction. "As has been noted by many observers over the past 100 years, Americans are anxious, confused, ambivalent, and guilt-ridden in their attitudes toward beverage alcohol," says Anderson. "We are said to be a culture divided among the wets, the drys, and the damp deniers of the controversy."[43]

Today, use of alcohol is still firmly embedded in the American way of life. Drinking has numerous applications, from religious sacraments to the two-martini lunch.

At the same time, we have no defined norms about what constitutes acceptable drinking. Drinking has not gained respectability, even though over half the people in the United States drink alcohol at least on occasion. The stigma attached to public drunkenness still runs deep, and alcoholics are still hidden away in jails, workhouses, and prisons. Oversimplifying a bit, we can say that our attitude toward drinking has two distinct poles: We love it, and we loathe it.

Our use of language reveals the latter. We will go to almost any length to avoid speaking plainly about someone being drunk. In fact, English offers us a rich legacy of terminology to describe intoxication. As early as 1733, Benjamin Franklin noted this and published a list of such terms in the *Pennsylvania Gazette* as "The Drinker's Dictionary." Among the synonyms for intoxication were the following:

> He is Addled.
>
> He's casting up his Accounts.
>
> His head is full of Bees.
>
> He sees the Bears.
>
> He's Cherry Merry.
>
> He's Loaded his Cart.
>
> He's Seafaring.
>
> He's got his Top Gallant Sails out.
>
> He's seen a Flock of Moons.
>
> He's Religious.[44]

Our situation today is still much the same. As historian Alice Fleming describes in her book *Alcohol: The Delightful Poison*, "People hesitate to talk openly about things they do not understand, and drunkenness has been, and still is, one of those things."[45]

CHAPTER TWO

The Minnesota Model is Born—
˙ Three Crucial Experiments

During the late 1940s and early 1950s, Minnesota was the location of three experiments in chemical dependency treatment. This statewide laboratory had three centers: Pioneer House in Minneapolis, Hazelden in the small rural town of Center City, and Willmar State Hospital. Their efforts gave us the perspectives and practices known today as the Minnesota Model.

In each experiment, the architects of the model faced the old stigma surrounding alcoholism. Their initial efforts, recalls Daniel Anderson, took place against a background of "deep gloom and pessimism."[1] At that time, AA was the new kid on the treatment block—either ignored or dismissed. Most of the general public simply didn't know that the group existed. Many psychologists saw alcoholism as a symptom of some deeper, underlying disorder, and regarded the spirituality of the program with skepticism. Members of the clergy often held AA in suspicion, too, fearing that it was a religious rival.

At the time, hospitals still routinely refused to admit alcoholics. Lynn Carroll, Hazelden's first director, recalled an incident from 1940:

> They would not take an alcoholic into any hospital that
> I know of at that time—I remember at one time that I
> was down to Mankato [Minnesota], and was doing quite

a lot of drinking. I went up to a Catholic hospital and wanted to get in and they told me to sit down. Then the priest came down and told me to get the hell out of there or he'd call the police. That's what they used to think of the alcoholic.[2]

Pioneer House, Hazelden, and Willmar State Hospital were among the first programs to revolt against the cultural tide and win acceptance. Pioneer House received its initial backing from the city welfare department in 1948. Hazelden was the brainchild of a group of business people who privately funded its first program in 1949. Willmar was unique because its innovations in alcoholism treatment took place in the midst of a mainstream health care institution. However, all three programs were deeply rooted in the philosophy and practices of AA, discovering there a potent force for personal change.

CRONIN SHAPES PIONEER HOUSE

Patrick Cronin was the first recorded person in Minnesota to gain sobriety through AA. It happened this way:

In early summer 1940, Cronin read a review of the Big Book, the basic text of AA. He wrote the General Service Office of AA in New York to find out more. Unfortunately, there was no local AA chapter in Minneapolis, so the office suggested that Cronin contact a fellowship in Chicago.

On November 9, 1940, to Cronin's surprise, two AA members from Chicago showed up at his door. They had expected to stay only one day, but those plans quickly changed when a blizzard tied up traffic and closed businesses in Minneapolis for three days. That gave the two visitors an opportunity to "work" on Cronin for four full days, grounding him in the ideas of AA.

It worked. November 11, 1940, was Cronin's "dry date," and he remained a sober member of AA for the rest of his life. Soon after saying good-bye to his visitors, Cronin joined a small group of other men who gathered to discuss how they could stay sober. But when Cronin rented a building in Minneapolis with the purpose of forming an AA club, he was surprised by the opposition he faced. Glenn Farmer, later a director of Pioneer House, recalls the incident: "They rented this building, and then the neighbors found out that there was going to be a house full of drunks and drunks lying all over the streets, sidewalks, and lawns. The idea had to be abandoned."[3]

The Relief Department of the city of Minneapolis was more agreeable. In 1948 it offered Cronin a place at one of its branches, Mission Farms, to hold AA meetings and accommodate people who wanted to stay overnight. In 1949 the department formally hired Cronin as a counselor at Mission Farms.

During that year 189 people were admitted to Mission Farms for alcoholism treatment. Farmer remembers that in those days there was no medically supervised procedure for detoxification. He recalls sitting on one alcoholic's chest for four hours to prevent that person from falling out of bed from the d.t.'s (delirium tremens).[4]

The program for alcoholics found temporary quarters in several places at Mission Farms, including buildings known as the "Ice House" and the "Winter Quarters." Another short-lived home was "Little Mother's Inn," which burned down in 1953.

Cronin's program moved to a more permanent home in a potato warehouse, a stone building that stored the ample crop of that vegetable grown on the 437 acres of Mission Farms. It took weeks of volunteer work by local AA members to dig out the dirt and create some usable space. Soon after that, someone erected a sign outside the warehouse bearing the words "Pioneer House." That was the program's official christening, and the name stuck.

Under Cronin, Pioneer House became the first AA-based treatment center in Minnesota. Each resident at Pioneer House received a copy of the Big Book and another staple of AA literature, *Twelve Steps and Twelve Traditions*. This has since become a common practice at treatment programs based on the Minnesota Model.

The Twelve Steps formed the core of the program at Pioneer House. Cronin placed special emphasis on completing Steps Four and Five, those that call for alcoholics to take a "searching and fearless moral inventory" and share the results of that inventory with another person. "You either did those [Steps] or you got to stay there forever," recalls Glenn Farmer.[5]

Cronin's lectures on the Steps were another mainstay of the program, though he admitted there was nothing sacred in his understanding of AA. "There are no official, dogmatic interpretations of the Twelve Steps by anyone in the entire organization," Cronin noted. "From the founders to the newcomer, each man works out his own philosophy of life using the Twelve Steps as guides along the way." Cronin also stressed that AA was a program put together "by drunks for drunks." Thus it stood outside the medical mainstream represented by physicians, psychiatrists, and psychologists.[6]

The AA program hinged on Step One, Cronin explained—the admission of powerlessness over alcohol. He added that the founders of AA knew they would never exact any promise from alcoholics about never drinking again. Instead the Steps offer a list of suggestions for changing the mental states that *precipitate* drinking: chief among them being resentment, self-pity, fear, and remorse. Ultimately, the Steps are about finding a source of outside help—a "Higher Power"—to change those thoughts and attitudes.

"There are no half-measures here," said Cronin. "We must make a complete surrender to the simple fact that, using the tools we possess, we cannot manage our lives if we continue the use of alcohol in any form." Cronin also noted that alcoholics recoil when their thinking and behavior are described as insane. But, he reminded his listeners, [if I] "had a movie camera with a soundtrack and followed them for a day while they were spinning, they might well doubt their sanity when they witnessed some of the silly, comic, tragic, vicious things they did while temporarily insane."[7]

Other excerpts from Cronin's talks convey the way he explained the practical psychology of AA to the residents at Pioneer House:

> There's a very simple way to stay dry the rest of your life without using any spiritual program to do it. Go out and cold-bloodedly kill somebody. The state will lock you up for the rest of your natural life and you won't have to bother about beating the booze; the warden will do that for you. . . .
>
> Unless happiness accompanies sobriety, your period of dryness will be short-lived. Every man is entitled to happiness; so are those with whom we have to live. . . .
>
> In your meditations, try to realize the millions and millions of men and women, down through the ages, who have died from alcoholism. Also meditate on the fact that, out of the estimated four million alcoholics in this country, you have been chosen as one of the pioneers in being exposed to the AA way of life. . . .
>
> If a man were promised complete relief from cancer of the liver, provided he made a complete, honest inventory of his moral assets and liabilities, don't you think he would be quite thorough about the job? What's stopping you? You've got cancer of the soul. . . .
>
> Don't forget to include yourself in the list of people you have harmed. We have outraged our bodies, confused our minds, and lost our self-respect. We owe ourselves complete restitution in all these areas. . . .
>
> In each of the Steps we are advised to *do* something. Not sit supinely in the Everlasting Arms and expect the love of God to do everything for us. Each Step calls for action on our part."[8]

Today Pioneer House, now called Hazelden Center for Youth and Families, is owned by Hazelden and offers services for chemically dependent adolescents. Yet it will also be remembered as the birthplace of AA-based treatment in Minnesota, a program that helped alcoholics from the streets of Minneapolis turn their lives around.

HAZELDEN: "AN ASYLUM FOR ALCOHOLICS OF THE PROFESSIONAL CLASS"

Richard Coyle Lilly was a financier and philanthropist who had the reputation of being a "hard drinker" and a "hard-nosed banker." He was also the stuff of legends. One of the surviving stories about him has a direct bearing on the origins of the Minnesota Model.

One night, while Lilly was driving home from a poker game and drinking bout, he had a near-fatal accident. His car careened off St. Paul's High Bridge, which spanned the Mississippi River, and landed on a barge full of sand. Miraculously, Lilly's life was spared. The event convinced Lilly to stop drinking and devote his prodigious wealth and talent to working with other alcoholics.

In 1947, Lilly bought the Powers Estate, some farmland near Center City, Minnesota, through the Coyle Foundation. He then re-sold the land to a group of Minneapolis-St. Paul businessmen who wanted to create a new treatment center for alcoholics. On January 10, 1949, Hazelden incorporated as a "charitable hospital corporation."

In its beginnings, as a guest house for alcoholic businessmen, Hazelden concentrated on the principles of AA. In this respect it echoed Cronin's work at Pioneer House. And like Pioneer House, Hazelden's facilities were modest: a farmhouse populated by three staff members and an average daily population of seven patients.

In *Hazelden: A Spiritual Odyssey*, Damian McElrath notes that Hazelden's early program hinged on four key expectations: that patients "practice responsible behavior," "attend the lectures on the Steps," "associate and talk with the other patients," and "make their beds."[9] Added to these was another rule: "Never allow a guy to sit around and mope."[10]

You could dismiss this simple list of rules as primitive, the first faltering attempts of a new treatment center. Yet behind this simple list was a rich body of intuitive wisdom and clinical savvy. Hazelden's founders agreed with AA that the major thrust of the practicing alcoholic's life is self-aggrandizement—"self-will run riot," as the Big Book describes it. McElrath notes that Hazelden's rules prompted patients to shift from a life of isolation to a life of dialogue. "The underlying principle," writes McElrath, "is that recovery takes place with one alcoholic talking to another over a cup of coffee."[11]

Three other elements were key to Hazelden's program during the early 1950s: AA principles, serene surroundings, and the resident counselor as a role model. The underlying idea was to create a separate therapeutic community for alcoholics, a core feature of the Minnesota Model.

Many alcoholics who left treatment were homeless and jobless. Responding to this need, Hazelden established Fellowship Club, a halfway house, in 1953. Hazelden also founded Dia Linn, a treatment center for women, in 1956. This was an innovation, since the stigma faced by women addicts was more profound than that faced by men.

A pivotal event in Hazelden's history was its hiring of Daniel Anderson as director in 1961. Anderson, one of the architects of alcoholism treatment at Willmar State Hospital, brought something new to the AA-based program at Hazelden: working knowledge of a multidisciplinary approach to the treatment of alcoholism. And just as it had at Pioneer House and Hazelden, the program at Willmar emerged from a series of happy "accidents."

BRADLEY UNLOCKS THE DOORS
AND REVOLUTIONIZES TREATMENT

History turns on small events. Who knows where the Minnesota Model would be today if Nelson Bradley's car hadn't broken down in the Twin Cities one day in 1947.

Bradley, a medical student, set out from Saskatchewan for a Michigan hospital to complete the last year of his surgical residency.

After his car broke down, he decided instead to finish his medical training in Minnesota. After his schooling, he took a job at the state hospital in Hastings. There Bradley met Daniel Anderson, who was then an attendant. While at Hastings, Anderson and Bradley worked under Dr. Ralph Rossen, the hospital's superintendent. Rossen operated from a simple philosophy that focused on "each single day in the life of a patient, always trying to improve the quality of that life."[12]

In 1950 Bradley became the superintendent at Willmar State Hospital, taking Anderson with him as recreation director, the only job opening available at that time. Willmar was the original and only state hospital in Minnesota required to admit "inebriates." It was also a state hospital for the mentally ill. Putting these two populations together was not unusual, since alcoholism was seen as being closely linked with mental illness. In fact, places like Willmar were often described as "snake pits."[13] And the professionals who worked in them soon confronted the phenomenon of derived stigma. Not only were alcoholics ostracized; those who tried to help alcoholics were suspect too.

The staff at Willmar questioned its way of treating alcoholics for a simple reason: it didn't work. A high percentage of alcoholic patients refused to cooperate with the primarily custodial treatment offered at the hospital, and many of them returned to drinking.

Bradley decided to change all this. Shortly after arriving at Willmar, he recognized that nonpsychotic "inebriates" were different from mental patients and needed their own kind of treatment, whatever that was. He also unlocked the ward doors for all but the most disoriented mental and inebriate patients. Paradoxically, the escape rate of the previously uncooperative inebriate patients, which had been around 25 percent, dropped to around 6 percent.[14]

In another bold move, Bradley decided to hire recovering alcoholics as counselors to work with the alcoholics at Willmar. In 1954, the Minnesota Civil Service Commission approved Bradley's decision by creating the new position of Counselor on Alcoholism. Recovering members of AA could now join physicians, psychologists, social workers, and clergy in treatment efforts aimed at alcoholics and other drug abusers.

WILLMAR DEVELOPS A WORKING SET OF ASSUMPTIONS

The program at Willmar deserves special attention. It was the first of three programs mentioned in this chapter to use a multidisciplinary approach to treatment. It married the skills of clergy members, physicians, social workers, psychologists, and recovering counselors. The result was the blend of modern clinical psychology, medical care, and AA practices we now call the Minnesota Model.

For Daniel Anderson, the Minnesota Model consists of two basic elements: a list of perspectives about the nature of alcoholism, and a set of practices aimed at providing comprehensive treatment for alcoholics.[15] Today these perspectives and practices seem commonplace. In 1950, however, they were the stuff of revolution.

Willmar had a thirty-year history of providing custodial care for alcoholics. Its only "treatment" for alcoholism was a brief period of detoxification and a ticket to locked wards. In some cases, alcoholics were housed with patients diagnosed as psychotic, hardly an unusual practice in 1950.[16]

The impetus for changing all this, says Anderson, came when he and his colleagues at Willmar bought into a set of assumptions widely viewed as radical *and* unworkable:[17]

1. Alcoholism exists.
2. Alcoholism is an illness.
3. Alcoholism is a no-fault illness.
4. Alcoholism is a multiphasic illness.
5. Alcoholism is a chronic, primary illness.
6. Initial motivation for treatment is unrelated to outcome.

7. Education about alcoholism must begin in the community.

Alcoholism Exists

Alcoholism in 1950 had the double dubious distinction of being both devastating and hidden. Large numbers of people simply did not want to see or believe that the condition existed outside of skid row. And when it was admitted to public consciousness, alcoholism was explained away as a mere symptom — the outward expression of a yet-to-be-diagnosed disorder.

Daniel Anderson and his colleagues opposed this view with assumption number one: Alcoholism exists. Though the signs and symptoms of this illness have a variety of individual expressions, there is enough commonality among them to say they share a single entity: alcoholism. Even drinkers themselves can be trained to identify those symptoms. These people drink excessively — a fact that leads to sustained and harmful consequences. In addition, their best efforts to stop drinking have come to nothing.

Alcoholism Is a No-fault Illness

Assumptions number two and three stem from an observation: Alcoholic drinking behavior is rigid, repetitive, and inflexible. Left to their own devices, alcoholics simply cannot make sustained changes in the way they drink. Thus, it makes sense to label the condition as an involuntary disability. Accordingly, asking alcoholics to put the bottle away on their own is like asking a person with paralyzed legs to run a marathon, or asking a clinically depressed person to have a nice day. According to Anderson, loss of control over drinking paired with physical dependence on alcohol is the backbone of the disease concept of alcoholism.

Blaming, stigmatizing, and serving the alcoholic with repeated pleas to quit drinking — all these responses are useless. Moreover, they preclude even the possibility that addicts can get meaningful treatment.

Alcoholism Is a Multiphasic Illness

With assumption four, the Minnesota Model reaffirms an insight from AA. Members of that group often speak of alcoholism as a three-part disease: physical, mental, and spiritual. The physical effects of long-term alcoholism are well documented; sustained alcoholism can damage every organ system in the body. In addition, noted the founders of AA, the mental life of alcoholics is dominated by resentment, fear, and remorse over harms done to others as a result of drinking. This prompts alcoholics to further isolate themselves and hide or deny the facts and consequences about their drinking.

All this adds up to a malady that AA labels spiritual: Alcoholics stubbornly refuse to transcend themselves. They have an almost supernatural belief in their ability to manage, or stop, their drinking, in spite of all evidence to the contrary. As a result, they refuse to admit their limitations and accept help.

The term *spiritual* has many meanings, yet the spiritual traditions of the world concur on one fact: that human beings suffer and need help from a source outside themselves. According to the Big Book, alcoholics begin recovery when they admit this fact and reach out to a source of help that transcends their current understanding.

Alcoholism, then, has effects that ripple through all dimensions of life. The alcoholic is often impaired physically, emotionally, and socially.

Thus the Minnesota Model of treatment was "holistic" long before that term became fashionable. The alliance with AA prevented the founders of the Minnesota Model from seeing the alcoholic as a bundle of isolated symptoms. From the beginning, the model aimed to treat the whole person—physical, emotional, and spiritual. In everyday terms, this meant that treatment programs could bring together the expertise of people in many disciplines: physicians, psychiatrists, clinical psychologists, social workers, counselors, members of the clergy, and even recovering people.

Alcoholism Is a Chronic, Primary Illness

With assumption five came another practice that shattered the status quo in 1950: the decision to treat alcoholism as a *primary* illness. Alcoholics commonly enter treatment with an array of problems. Yet it makes sense to focus initial treatment efforts on one problem above all: the addiction to alcohol or other drugs.

Yes, alcoholics are often anxious, depressed, or riddled with symptoms of physical illness. Conventional wisdom would start with the physical or emotional symptoms with the help of a counselor or physician. Anderson and his colleagues, however, simply chose to focus on alcoholism as their starting point. This made sense, they reasoned, even though drinking may have been initially triggered by some distressing event: a failed relationship, a lost job, or some other life crisis. But once set in motion, pathological drinking becomes an "autonomous drive"—a concern that takes the place of all others.

For example, alcoholics are often preoccupied with acquiring, maintaining, and consuming their liquor supplies. Eventually their thinking and actions take on a circular quality. At one time, perhaps, these people drank because they were anxious, lonely, or depressed. Eventually, however, their drinking became a chronic behavior that took on a life of its own.

The decision to treat alcoholism as a primary, chronic disease was pragmatic. In 1950 there was no extensive body of theoretical or empirical literature to guide treatment efforts. Bradley, Anderson, and their colleagues instead acted on a kind of enlightened, flying-by-the-seat-of-the-pants attitude: "What's being done with alcoholics now simply isn't working, so try something different." Their experience told them that little progress could be made in dealing with other problems until the alcoholic abstained.

Anderson and his colleagues also abandoned the idea that alcoholism could be cured. Instead, they chose to view alcoholism as a chronic illness, one that calls for long-term caring, not short-term curing. This decision was also made on pragmatic grounds: they could see no evidence of "cured" alcoholics. Instead, they concentrated on teaching alcoholics how to live with the condition for a lifetime—an orientation based on coping rather than curing. Returning to "social," or controlled, drinking was not an option. Abstinence was the goal of recovery, with relapse viewed as an undesirable but not unexpected outcome.

Here the staff at Willmar borrowed the "one day at a time" philosophy of AA: the aim for the recovering alcoholic was to avoid taking a drink for the next twenty-four hours. This seemed far more reasonable to the patients than the thought of abstaining for a lifetime.

Initial Motivation for Treatment Is Unrelated to Outcome

In 1950, the prevailing view held that patient motivation was closely related to favorable treatment outcome. In other words, before alcoholics could be helped, they had to *want* help. Anderson and colleagues turned the notion around: they assumed that initial motivation for treatment had no relation to treatment outcome. In fact, the alcoholics who entered Willmar were often noted for their defiance and resistance to treatment. Through a treatment program guided by the seven assumptions listed above, however, many of these same drinkers achieved sustained sobriety.

Anderson notes that research on treatment outcomes conducted at Willmar during the late 1950s showed only a modest success rate: 27 to 34 percent of alcoholics stayed sober. Yet alcoholics referred by the courts for mandatory treatment—people expected to resist treatment the most—did as well as those who entered treatment voluntarily. Anderson explains, "The conclusion we had to draw was simply that almost all alcoholics are probably locked in resistance and that few initially are able to admit and accept their alcoholism."[18]

Education About Alcoholism Must Begin in the Community

Anderson and his colleagues were buoyed by their discovery that motivation and treatment outcome were separate issues. Moreover, they hoped the local community would meet the new treatment program with enthusiasm. Those hopes were quickly dashed. In fact, Anderson recalls, community members used defense mechanisms much like those favored by alcoholics themselves. Even in the face of conflicting evidence, people on the other side of the hospital doors often chose to ignore alcoholism or insist that alcoholics were moral reprobates.

In response, the staff at Willmar began community education programs aimed mainly at the alcoholic's family members and employers. These programs offered straightforward information about the signs and symptoms of alcoholism. Anderson hoped this would help people see through the predominant assumptions about alcoholism and encourage anyone in the early stages of problem drinking to get help: "Without the involvement of family and friends, without their awareness, understanding, and encouragement to action, we would never be able to motivate most alcoholics to seek treatment."[19]

CHEMICAL DEPENDENCY EMBRACES MULTIPLE FORMS OF ADDICTION

By 1950 Willmar was admitting people addicted to narcotics as well as alcohol. All these people were then referred to as "inebriates." Here conventional wisdom, which labeled alcoholics and other addicts with the same pejorative term, hinted at a useful idea. As long as all types of addicts were lumped together in the same hospital wards, why not treat them together? Support for this came from an observation made not only at Willmar but at Hazelden and Pioneer House in the late 1950s: More people were entering treatment with more than one addiction.

Anderson and his colleagues began using a new term that broadly defined these dual addictions: *chemical dependency.* This was the beginning of a theoretical framework that could embrace all mind-altering substances. This new view acknowledged that people could be addicted to several chemicals at once, or several in succession. The term *cross-addiction* reminds us of this—that people who have been addicted to one chemical can be vulnerable to others as well. Beyond this, the new notion of chemical dependency led treatment professionals to conclude that alcoholics and other addicts could be successfully treated in the same setting.[20]

SEEING THE POWER OF AA

All these assumptions produced a treatment program that aimed at caring instead of curing. Added to this was the presence of a therapeutic community, the talents of a multidisciplinary staff, and a liberal dose of AA philosophy.

The staff at Willmar was initially skeptical about the latter element. Anderson recalls his early misgivings: AA seemed to call for motivation on the part of the alcoholic, meaning drinkers had to be willing to attend meetings. Anderson also worried that AA believers might seem too dogmatic to a practicing alcoholic. Besides, among the few people who had heard of the program, AA had the reputation of being fanatical, almost cult-like.

Anderson's thinking changed after he began meeting with local AA members over coffee. The spirit he found in these people came directly from the admonitions of the Big Book: Don't preach to other alcoholics; just share your experience. And don't push the "God-talk"; let each person choose his or her own conception of a Higher Power.

There were other facts Anderson observed. For one, members of AA were enjoying periods of extended sobriety. These people talked about their experiences in a way that meshed with Willmar's new assumptions about alcoholism. Moreover, AA members could do more than talk. They also volunteered to work directly with alcoholics in treatment. Eventually Anderson and Bradley concluded that this strange new movement, founded by alcoholics to help other alcoholics, was worthy of becoming a staple of Willmar's program.[21]

WILLMAR SHAPES ITS DAILY PROGRAM

Once they managed to get alcoholics into treatment, Anderson and his colleagues faced another problem: what to *do* with these people on a daily basis. A chronic scarcity of funds and trained staff complicated this decision even more.

The solution they adopted had two dimensions: First, make the total treatment environment therapeutic—one in which almost every event would prompt alcoholics to change the ways they thought, felt, and acted. Because alcoholism is multidimensional, affecting every aspect of the alcoholic's life, treatment has to take on a similar quality.

Second, allow alcoholics to help each other. Through informal conversations unsupervised by professional staff, patients could share their stories. Drinkers and addicts of every religious or political persuasion and socioeconomic class could discover what they had in common: lives severely disrupted by alcohol or other drugs. This led to an observation made by many practitioners of the Minnesota Model: *the real healing begins after the treatment staff goes home.* Allowing chemically dependent people to help one another triggers a powerful therapeutic process: *identification.* This is the "aha" experience people get when they come to the conclusion *I'm not alone. What's happened to me has happened to other people, too.*

To make the therapeutic community even more powerful, Anderson and his colleagues removed alcoholics from the mental wards and created a separate treatment area for them. This made the environment even more intensive and promoted greater interaction between patients.

Making this happen called for an informal environment, one that dissolved old barriers between professionals and patients. Anderson recalled what it was like: "Patients and staff alike were called by their first names; drinking experiences and alcoholic histories were dramatically revealed at the slightest provocation; suggestions were freely given based on one's own experiential background of alcoholism—and recovery; enthusiasm was openly expressed about the good prospects most patients had for recovery; and coffee was consumed extensively throughout the day and night."[22] The casual environment at Willmar prompted trust and radical self-disclosure.

But there was more to the program than informal exchange between patients. Patients attended small group sessions, usually led by recovering alcoholic counselors. Many of the small groups focused on a specific task for recovery drawn from the principles of AA: overcoming resentment, making amends, and more. Patients often formed their own peer groups even when no staff member was available to lead them. Anderson notes that this was a direct example of the helper-therapy principle: those who help others also help themselves. "We could now emancipate the alcoholic patient from the traditional passive-dependent-patient relationship and, in effect, let each patient play a more active and involved role in helping another patient."[23]

Soon after beginning small group sessions, the staff at Willmar noticed a by-product of this process: the counselors on alcoholism spontaneously delivered informal "lectures" about the nature of alcoholism and Twelve Step recovery. Seeing the effect these talks were having, Anderson and his colleagues lent their official blessing to the idea: they started a lecture series for patients. Soon these lectures were offered daily and attended by everyone in treatment.

The lecture series at Willmar violated some official canons of learning theory. The openly didactic lectures were criticized as an inefficient and outdated way to deliver information. Still, the new theories about lectures did not take into account the treatment environment. Alcoholics attending a lecture appeared to be passive listeners. Yet when they heard about the signs and symptoms of alcoholism, the members could quietly identify with what the speaker was saying—all in the anonymous safety of the lecture hall. During a lecture, alcoholics gained a new perspective on their behavior without having to confess the details of their personal lives or face public ridicule.[24]

Not all the treatment experiences at Willmar took place in groups, however. Patients were also paired with counselors for one-on-one sessions, ideally with recovering people of the same sex and age. An alternative to formal counseling, these sessions offered patients a chance to get individualized coaching from a role model—another alcoholic or addict who was managing to stay sober. Anderson notes that the counselors also became patient advocates, moving heaven and earth when necessary to provide needed services for their clients.[25] These lay counselors were people whose main qualification for working in a hospital was their own alcoholism. Anderson recalls how difficult it was at first for the hospital staff to accept the new counselors on alcoholism. Soon, however, these counselors were delivering most of the direct services to the patients at Willmar.[26]

Patients also got work assignments—jobs in the library, laundry, kitchen, or maintenance shop. None of these tasks were glamorous, but they provided a therapeutic revelation: alcoholic patients discovered they could work constructively for six or seven hours each day. In the process, they could not only stay sober but help to maintain the hospital.

At a time when managed care companies press for reduced treatment stays, it is good to reflect on the Willmar treatment model from 1950. When Anderson and his colleagues designed a sixty-day program for alcoholics, they encountered a common reaction: such a length of stay was far too short, critics said. Little or nothing could be accomplished in such time.[27] That reaction seems understandable given the prevailing method of alcohol treatment at that time: ignoring alcoholics or consigning them to institutional care for months or even years.

The shortened length of stay was further incentive to treat chemical dependency as a primary condition. Given the more limited time frame, Willmar staff simply chose to forget about probing their patients' psyches for any underlying "causes" of drinking. Instead, they harnessed strategies for helping alcoholics modify their behavior immediately.

Another innovation in treatment has already been touched on: use of a multidisciplinary staff. Again, few people were trained to work with alcoholics in 1950. Even fewer *wanted* to do so. Despite this, Willmar merged the talents of physicians, social workers, psychologists, nurses, members of the clergy, and psychiatric aides.

Treatment at Willmar included another element now considered essential for Minnesota Model treatment: individualized treatment planning. Working together, the whole staff devised a plan for each patient. Anderson remembers how heated some of those first meetings were. Staff members disagreed about almost everything, then gradually learned to speak each other's professional language and appreciate each other's insights.

Members of the clergy also found a place on the treatment staff. Originally, they listened to patients complete their Fifth Step. Gradually the clergy took on other roles as well, including general counseling.

The assumptions and program structure used by many Minnesota Model programs today are much like those developed at Willmar. The model has two basic aims: to promote abstinence, not only from alcohol, but from all mind-altering chemicals; and to help the patient unlearn a self-destructive lifestyle.[28]

How do we know when patients have met these two goals and are ready to be discharged? Willmar's answer was to discharge patients when the staff felt they were ready for the next stage of growth—the next step in the continuum of care. In some cases, this meant returning home and attending AA meetings. In other cases, it meant going to a halfway house, outpatient treatment, or to individual counseling for a psychological condition. Needless to say, aftercare planning is an important part of the Minnesota Model.[29]

Anderson speculates that much of the success enjoyed by a Minnesota Model program might come from one feature: infusing a treatment program with the spirit of mutual help found in AA. He writes:

> The profound implication here is that if one can accept oneself as limited, if one can give up trying to be omnipotent, it is from this very admission of limitation that one can give to, and contribute to, other limited human beings. It is from this limitation that one can join the human race and find a common mutual humanity. [30]

SUMMING UP

Any discussion about the specifics of the early programs at Willmar, Hazelden, and Pioneer House must be rounded out with a reminder about how radical their approaches were at the time. The staff at these facilities had the audacity to suggest that alcoholics were worth treating and were actually capable of change. Set this against the ideological backdrop of the late 1940s and early 1950s: the widespread stigma attached to alcoholism and the prevailing view that drunkenness was a product of moral inferiority, not illness.

Those who criticize specific treatment methods or success rates for chemical dependency treatment centers often forget this larger perspective. With its assertions about the dignity and worth of the alcoholic and addict, the Minnesota Model represented a social reform movement of real magnitude.

Chapter Three

Understanding the Minnesota Model

There is nothing truly original about the Minnesota Model of chemical dependency treatment. Nearly everything used in it has been borrowed or adapted from another source. Didactic lectures, cognitive-behavioral psychology, AA principles, bibliotherapy—all these elements and many more became part of that synthesis we call the Minnesota Model. Even the designation *Minnesota Model* is arbitrary. At other times it has aptly been called the *Willmar Model* or the *Hazelden Model*. Like all creative acts, the originality of the model comes not from creating new elements but from juxtaposing and mixing existing elements in a new way. The model is a classic example of American pragmatism.

Three Core Perspectives

Though the Minnesota Model is flexible and widely adopted, it presents a unique perspective on treatment. We could even reduce the seven assumptions behind the model listed in chapter 2 to three core perspectives:

- Treat people with chemical dependency.
- Treat them with dignity.
- Treat them as whole persons—body, mind, and spirit.

Treat People with Chemical Dependency

The survey presented in chapters 1 and 2 illustrates how rare this perspective is historically. Over the last two millennia, the most common responses to chemically dependent people have included ignoring them, punishing them, locking them in mental wards or jails, or offering them temperance lectures. The idea that such people deserve humane treatment is a surprisingly recent invention—one that has been widely practiced only in this century.

Treat Them with Dignity

Supporting all the disciplines used in the model is an unshakable commitment to treat every alcoholic and addict with dignity and respect. The overriding message is this: *You will not be judged here. You are welcome. You are one of us.*

Treat Them as Whole Persons—Body, Mind, and Spirit

The first two perspectives listed above present the Minnesota Model as a movement for social reform. Equally important is the model's clinical aspect, the subject of the third assumption.

But if alcoholism is a condition with many levels, why not respond on an equal number of levels? The Minnesota Model does just that. It grew from a fortunate marriage of the program of AA, the tools of modern clinical psychology, and medical science. Implicit in these elements is a concern for the holistic dimension of human life: body, mind, and spirit.

Expressed in more academic terms, this is called a *physical-psycho-spiritual* model. First, patients receive needed medical care—immediate attention to the often severe physical consequences of addiction. Included here are medical assessment and detoxification.

Second, people who experience Minnesota Model treatment work at the intellectual level. They are armed with a new set of ideas about the nature of their disease of chemical dependency. Beyond this, they learn new strategies for changing their mental habits—

what AA calls the "stinking thinking" that fuels addiction. This aspect of the model borrows from the contributions of cognitive-behavioral psychotherapy, a prime example being the Rational-Emotive Therapy developed by Albert Ellis.

Third, people in treatment learn the necessity of living their lives on a spiritual level. This part of the Minnesota Model is the most difficult to explain scientifically, yet it may be the most powerful part of the overall program. Learning to live at a spiritual level involves acknowledging one's personal limitations, vulnerabilities, and need for the help that other people can offer. It includes a relationship with a Higher Power that is individually defined. Spirituality is kept alive through the daily practice of prayer and meditation and a day-by-day effort to purge the mind of the mental conditions that contribute to addiction. Among these conditions are resentment, fear, and remorse over harm done to others.

The Minnesota Model led to visible changes in the daily practice of addiction treatment. Professionals who once had little direct contact with each other found themselves walking the same wards. These include physicians, psychologists, members of the clergy, recovering people, recreation specialists, nutritionists—even massage therapists and acupuncturists. One of the lasting contributions of the Minnesota Model is that it forced professionals to break down their customary walls of isolation and talk to each other.

In Not-God, Ernest Kurtz discusses AA's insistence that alcoholism is a three-part disease: physical, mental, and spiritual. Every event in our lives resonates on those three levels.[1] The core of the Minnesota Model is a concerted attempt to respond to whole persons in all their messy, unscientific complexity, and to treat them with dignity.

THE MINNESOTA MODEL FOCUSES ON REHABILITATION

According to proponents of the Minnesota Model, the approach that most effectively responds to our threefold nature is rehabilitation. This approach has several key components:

- *Treatment professionals and patients collaborate in defining the path of recovery.* Their relationship goes beyond the usual patient-professional dichotomy. There is a give-and-take quality to the relationship, and the ideas of both professional and patient receive serious consideration. For example, physicians coordinate treatment and medical benefits; they also advise the patient about how to manage the illness on a day-by-day basis. Underlying all of this, however, is the expectation that people will take an active role in their own recovery.

- *Changes in lifestyle habits become the focus of treatment.* This can involve both behavioral and cognitive strategies.

- *Treatment focuses on the long-term.* In rehabilitation care, there is little expectation that the patient will walk away from treatment cured by a mysterious "magic bullet." As with treatment for lower-back pain or diabetes, the Minnesota Model works with problems that don't go away. The focus is on managing the condition, and living well with it. Any focus on cure is replaced with a sense of progress. Central to this are questions about the overall quality of life, issues that usually go well beyond the dynamics of medical cure.

- *Treatment is multidisciplinary.* Family relationships, finances, physical health—all can be damaged by addiction to alcohol or other mind-altering drugs. This collection of problems demands the expertise of professionals in medicine and mental health, along with the wisdom and practical experience of recovering alcoholics and other addicts.

- *Rehabilitation relies on natural support systems.* Family members, friends, and self-help groups all participate in the recovery process. Over time, patients loosen their ties to health care professionals. They take over more responsibility for managing their daily lives and using community resources.

Contrast the rehabilitation model with some defining features of the traditional medical model:

- *Patients are passive.* Their most important task is to follow the instructions. Physicians are far more active and control the content and duration of treatment.
- *Medications and surgery are the most common tools for treatment.* The illness or injury is treated as a physical condition; thus the body is severed from mind and spirit.
- *Treatment focuses on cure.* The focus is on short-term cure, rather than long-term care.

Treatment for alcoholism and drug addiction does not fit well into the world of the medical model. The rehabilitative model is a far more powerful tool for working with chemically dependent people. People living with addiction face many of the same daily tasks and existential dilemmas as people living with hypertension, diabetes, asthma, and other chronic illnesses. This is not meant to imply that the traditional medical model is "bad," only that it has limitations in treating conditions such as chemical dependency.

THE MINNESOTA MODEL AND THE TWELVE STEPS

Anderson acknowledges the special debt the developers of the Minnesota Model owe to Alcoholics Anonymous. "Without the initial and sustaining impetus of this self-help group," he writes, "none of our treatment efforts could have been realized."[2]

THE MINNESOTA MODEL CONTRASTS WITH OTHER MODELS

The Minnesota Model is not the only approach used in working with chemically dependent people. It competes with other, more exclusive models of treatment.

Detoxification

The Comprehensive Alcohol Abuse and Alcoholism Prevention, Treatment, and Rehabilitation Act of 1970 was a pivotal event in the history of American chemical dependency treatment. This act decriminalized public drunkenness. No longer were law enforcement officials required to arrest "inebriates" and warehouse them in jails. Instead, the law mandated that states replace criminal punishment of alcoholics with humane treatment programs, beginning with detoxification.

The first goal of any detox center, however, is to make physical withdrawal from an addictive drug safer. Detoxification is only one part of the Minnesota Model. Yet detoxification centers can provide a surprising variety of services: medical assessment, psychological evaluation, referral to further treatment or aftercare programs, vocational rehabilitation, AA sessions, hypnosis, acupuncture, and even programs for controlled drinking.

Psychotherapy

The psychotherapeutic, or psychiatric, model advocates group or individual counseling as the primary mode for treating addiction. Advocates of this approach often claim that addiction is merely a symptom of an underlying, more fundamental disorder.

It's easy to see why this model originally appealed to professionals in health care: alcoholism can mimic almost any psychological disorder. Many alcoholics and addicts report overwhelming feelings of anxiety, inferiority, depression, and other mood disorders. According to the psychotherapeutic model, these feelings are responses to life stress. The therapist's job is to root out the underlying stressful condition, thereby eliminating the patient's need for addictive chemicals.

Three factors consistently undermine this approach to treatment. First, drugs are, at times, used to assist with the therapeutic process. This introduces an added risk: dependence on prescribed drugs. Second, the length and cost of this kind of treatment rule it out as an option for many chemically dependent people. Third, anyone who relies on counseling as a primary mode of treatment soon bumps into a damnable difficulty. "With great frequency," notes Anderson, "alcoholics have a talent for sabotaging therapeutic relationships."[3] By 1950, psychiatrists and other mental health professionals largely acknowledged their ineffectiveness in treating alcoholism. Many simply lost interest in the problem. In fact, disillusionment with psychiatry was one of the forces that fueled the growth of AA and the Minnesota Model.

The Minnesota Model shares with psychoanalysis the goal of breaking through the addict's denial. Unlike psychoanalysis, however, the Minnesota Model does not call for scouring the addict's past to search out the "causes" of that person's drinking or drug use. Taking its lead from AA, practitioners of the Minnesota Model focus treatment on the present. Their goal is to help the addict or alcoholic take new actions *now*—specifically, to stay sober and clean for the next twenty-four hours.

Behavior Modification

Behavior modification includes any systematic attempt to manipulate the consequences of the addict's behavior. The goal is to reinforce abstinence or moderate drinking.[4]

When it comes to treating chemical dependency, behavior modification uses several strategies. One is to help people develop an aversion to mind-altering chemicals. Often this is accomplished by administering an electrical shock to people as they drink. Another strategy is to administer drugs, such as emetine, that produce nausea and vomiting when consumed with alcohol. Training in blood-alcohol discrimination training is a third option. Here drinkers are taught to monitor their level of intoxication at any given moment. The theory is simple: when patients know their blood alcohol concentration, they can take immediate steps to moderate their drinking. In addition, behaviorists often help patients learn systematic desensitization, that is, progressive relaxation exercises that lower anxiety in the face of stressful stimuli.

A prime example of behavior modification comes from the work of researchers Mark and Linda Sobell. In one study, the Sobells sought to teach a group of recovering alcoholics how to control their drinking. Toward that end, they created research settings designed to look like a living room and a bar. Subjects who ordered too many drinks in these environments received mild electrical shocks. They also used assertiveness training and role-playing as tools to learn how to moderate drinking.[4]

Today this method of treatment is difficult to find. And in the United States, research on controlled drinking has been abandoned, often on grounds that its lack of validity and reliability represents an unethical degree of risk for recovering alcoholics.

In contrast to behavior modification, the Minnesota Model calls on people in treatment to develop insight through lectures, reading assignments, and group therapy. Added to this is the program of action outlined by the Twelve Steps: taking a "fearless moral inventory," discussing the results of that inventory with others, making amends, working with a sponsor, learning how to meditate, and more. Because it emphasizes change in attitude as well as behavior, the Minnesota Model is much closer to cognitive-behavioral psychotherapy than to behavior modification or psychoanalysis.

The Emergent Model of Alcoholism

The Sobells, with E. Mansell Pattison, are the authors of *Emerging Concepts of Alcohol Dependence*. They advocate a new approach to treating alcoholism based on the following:[5]

1. *There is no single entity which can be defined as alcoholism.*

2. *There is no clear dichotomy between either alcoholics and nonalcoholics, or between prealcoholics and nonprealcoholics.*

3. *The developmental sequence of adverse consequences* [from alcoholism] *appears to be highly variable.*

4. *There is no clear evidence to date for a biological process that predetermines an individual toward dysfunctional use of alcohol.*

5. *The empirical evidence suggests that alcohol problems are reversible.*

6. *Alcohol problems are typically interrelated with other life problems.*

7. *It may be clinically useful to develop typologies of sub-populations for administrative program development.*

THE MINNESOTA MODEL AS A MIDDLE PATH

In *Easy Does It: Alcoholism Treatment Outcomes, Hazelden and the Minnesota Model*, author J. Clark Laundergan describes three models of alcoholism. One is the "emergent" model proposed by Pattison and the Sobells. He also discusses a "traditional" model and the Minnesota Model.

These three models contrast on each of the premises offered by the Sobells and Pattison. And on each point, the Minnesota Model takes a flexible and pragmatic middle path. It views alcoholism as a single entity, but at the same time recognizes the full range of individual differences among people with the condition of alcoholism.

When referring to individual drinking patterns, for example, reasonable people disagree about what constitutes "harmful consequences." Yet there is usually *enough* agreement about the destructiveness of these consequences to warrant treating alcoholism as a single entity even though its signs and symptoms differ widely among individual alcoholics.[6]

Anderson notes that elements of other models can be integrated into the Minnesota Model on an "as needed" basis. Examples include the use of Antabuse, which is a form of aversion therapy, or cognitive techniques such as relaxation training and assertiveness training.[7]

Given this flexibility, it's surprising that the Minnesota Model has been characterized as an inflexible, rigidly defined, lockstep approach to treatment. In reality, the model recognizes the vast differences between people in treatment and calls for individualized treatment planning. Yet even though individual differences exist, there is *enough* commonality between chemically dependent people to warrant treating them in the same setting. All chemically dependent people have experienced harmful consequences, even if those consequences differ in specifics. And all of them work in a group setting to make changes in their thinking and behavior, even though the specific content of those changes may differ.

In short, the Minnesota Model is a flexible approach that borrows freely from other sources. Flexibility and openness to change have been built into the model from the beginning. *The model grew from a simple, concrete focus on the well-being of alcoholics—not from the desire to forge an exclusive paradigm of treatment.* Toward that end, practitioners of the Minnesota Model draw on a kaleidoscope of treatment tools.

THE MINNESOTA MODEL—
PART OF A CONTINUUM OF CARE

The Minnesota Model is often mistakenly seen as being synonymous with inpatient treatment. To ensure that chemically dependent people receive appropriate services, the model actually calls for a wide-ranging continuum of care. In *Perspectives on Treatment,* Anderson lists the following services of that continuum:[8]

- *Diagnostic and referral centers.*
- *Detoxification centers.*
- *Inpatient treatment.*
- *Extended care programs.* Sometimes called *therapeutic communities,* these programs can last up to sixty days. Their aim is to help recovering people sustain the personal change they made during inpatient treatment. These programs focus on people who experience serious emotional or physical problems in addition to chemical dependency.
- *Residential intermediate care, also known as the "halfway house."* Here the purpose is to provide people with a surrogate family working the principles of recovery. Individual counseling and job placement are also typically part of this service.
- *Outpatient care.* Some recovering people enjoy enough physical

and emotional health to maintain their normal work and home lives during treatment. Outpatient services are ideal for them. These programs often mirror what's offered in primary residential care; the main difference is that outpatient care takes place on evenings or weekends.

- *Aftercare.* The most widely used aftercare resource is Alcoholics Anonymous. Individual counseling, family counseling, and other self-help groups are also options.

- *Family programs.* The addict's family members may unwittingly do things that enable the addiction to continue. Taking a cue from Al-Anon, these people "detach with love"—that is, stop making the alcoholic or addict the focus of their lives. Family members begin to see their powerlessness to control the addicted person; instead, they start attending to their own emotional, spiritual, and physical health.

THE MINNESOTA MODEL: FLEXIBLE, DYNAMIC, PRAGMATIC

Readers of *Perspectives on Treatment* might get the idea that the Minnesota Model evolved from a carefully derived theory. It did not. The model sprang from a mind-set best evoked by the phrases "Invent it as you go along" and "Do what works." What we now take as the basics of the Minnesota Model came from daily life in the trenches. These "basics" were often desperate attempts to make a difference in the lives of the people who walked through the doors at Willmar, Hazelden, and Pioneer House. The model's developers relied on trial and error. They did not proceed from rigorous research, or well-defined treatment protocols. In the late 1940s and early 1950s, none of these existed.

The Minnesota Model is based on practical perspectives, not prescriptions. This means that treatment according to the model can be delivered in a variety of settings: hospital-based or freestanding, profit or nonprofit. In any case, the presence of a multidisciplinary team of providers is a cornerstone of this approach. So is the program of AA. Beyond this, the model leaves ample room for future innovation.

SUMMING UP

As a movement of social reform, the Minnesota Model made three timeless contributions. First, it introduced the idea that chemically dependent people deserve treatment rather than isolation or abandonment in mental wards and prisons. Even a cursory review of history shows this attitude represented a radical departure from the past. Second, it held that chemically dependent people deserve to be treated with dignity, that their condition is the result of a disease in which personal volition plays a distinctly limited role. Finally, it operated on the premise that any effective addiction treatment must address the complex physical, mental, and spiritual aspects of that condition.

These assumptions were radical in 1950. And, as the history of treatment since 1950 indicates, they remain radical today.

CHAPTER FOUR

Progress and Problems—
1950 to 1990

SETTING THE STAGE: 1940-1950

Even before the crucial experiments in treatment were taking shape at real-life laboratories in Minnesota, research of a more academic kind was going on. During the 1940s, the Yale Center for Alcohol Studies became the first academic program in the United States to do serious research on alcoholism. Yale researchers started to grasp the multidimensional nature of alcoholism, view the condition as a disease, and call for interdisciplinary treatment.

Through publishing the *Quarterly Journal of Alcohol Studies,* the Yale Center became a major voice in the newly awakened dialogue about the nature of alcoholism and its treatment. The center also included a free clinic for alcoholics.

In 1943 the Yale Center began a summer school for the education of community leaders as well as the slowly developing treatment field. The goal of the school was to collect and communicate newfound knowledge about a variety of alcohol problems, including alcoholism itself. These schools continued each summer at Yale until 1962, and continued when the center moved to Rutgers State University of New Jersey.

Another milestone in the 1940s was the founding of the National Committee on Education on Alcoholism, which later became the National Council on Alcoholism (NCA). (It is known today as the

National Council on Alcoholism and Drug Dependence.) Marty Mann, a recovering woman, was the organization's first director. At that time the NCA estimated that there were five million alcoholics in America, and that most of them knew nothing of AA or any other kind of help for alcoholics. [1]

The essential question, said the NCA founders, was this: How can people learn that alcoholism exists, and that it is useful to view it as an illness? Moreover, how can we let them know that help is available and that alcoholics deserve help? The NCA's answer was to educate community leaders across the country about these issues and ask them to convince others. Their organization was to be a national agency comparable to the American Cancer Society or the American Lung Association. [2]

At its outset, most members of the NCA were recovering people or their immediate family members. Relatively few health care professionals joined. When asked about this, Mann offered a pointed reply: "You have to remember the early days of tuberculosis, [when] the only physicians you could get to work in TB wards were physicians who had it themselves or who had families who had tuberculosis. It's part of the stigma of alcoholism. It'll go away someday, but it's still with us." [3]

The 1940s also saw the creation of another national organization: the National States Conference on Alcoholism, which later became the Alcohol and Drug Problems Association (ADPA). Founded at the 1949 Yale summer school, the ADPA's purpose was to support changes in public policy regarding treatment of addicts and alcoholics. The ADPA worked to unify the advocacy efforts of various states and Canadian provinces.

Early on, the ADPA saw that one of the most pressing needs was for leadership from the federal government in diagnosing and treating alcoholism. Equally important, said the organization, were training treatment professionals and doing scientific research on alcoholism. In the United States, that research and treatment response would not come for another twenty years.

1950-1960

That brings us to the 1950s, which ushered in the birth of the Minnesota Model. Despite the presence of that model—along with AA, the Yale Center, and the new national organizations on alcoholism—popular attitudes toward alcoholics budged little. Hospitals across America were filled to capacity. In many cases there was literally no room in them, or in the emergency wards, for alcoholics. As Anderson recalls, it was possible to admit alcoholics into psychiatric wards. Yet there was a often a six-month waiting list even for these. In that time, the alcoholic could die.[4]

In 1956 the American Medical Association (AMA) lent its support to the movement to change the face of American alcoholism treatment. During that year it published a statement implicitly endorsing the disease concept of alcoholism by calling on hospitals to treat alcoholics. According to the AMA:

> Alcoholism must be regarded as within the purview of medical practice. The Council on Mental Health, its Committee on Alcoholism, and *the profession in general recognizes this syndrome of alcoholism as illness* which justifiably should have the attention of physicians.[5]

This statement was no mere academic pronouncement; it helped strike down another barrier for alcoholics, who were still regularly denied hospital beds and other urgent forms of medical care.

1960-1970

The 1950s ended with a limited expansion of treatment centers for alcoholism and of programs for training treatment providers. By the end of the decade there were perhaps two hundred small independent treatment programs in the United States.[6]

The 1960s were an intoxicating decade, a time of conflict and polarization around social issues such as the Vietnam War and civil rights. Added to this heady mixture of social change were two broad movements. First came a book on the disease concept of alcoholism written by a researcher affiliated with the Yale Center, E. M. Jellinek. Second was the growth of a counterculture that became widely linked with the use of illicit drugs.

Jellinek's book, *The Disease Concept of Alcoholism*, was a landmark in alcohol studies and is still widely quoted today. Yet even though Jellinek argued for viewing alcoholism and other drug addiction as a disease, he tempered his assertions with qualifications. He even hesitated to use the term *disease*, noting that the term *illness* might be more accurate. "It comes to this," he wrote, "that a *disease is what the medical profession recognizes as such.*"[7]

Jellinek defined alcoholism as "*any use of alcoholic beverages that causes any damage to the individual or society or both.*"[8] This definition is so expansive that some might dispute its value. Jellinek's answer is that that the definition is intentionally vague, forcing us to define more specific varieties of alcoholism. Jellinek then went on to identify five different types of alcoholism. He designated them with the first five letters of the Greek alphabet, seeking to avoid the negative connotations that more specific labels (such as *alcohol abuser* or *alcohol addict*) might bring.

Alpha alcoholism represents "purely psychological" dependence on the pain-reducing effect of alcohol. Jellinek referred to this as "undisciplined" or "problem" drinking, stating that it did not lead to loss of control or the inability to abstain. Even though this type of alcoholism can disrupt the drinker's family and work, he saw no signs that it represents a progressive illness with increasingly negative consequences.[9]

Beta alcoholism is more comprehensive than alpha alcoholism. With beta alcoholism come physical complications, such as gastritis, cirrhosis of the liver, and nutritional deficiencies. However, there are no withdrawal symptoms associated with this type of alcoholism.[10]

Jellinek defined *gamma alcoholism* as "that species of alcoholism in which (1) acquired increased tissue tolerance to alcohol, (2) adaptive cell metabolism . . ., (3) withdrawal symptoms and 'craving,' i.e., physical dependence, and (4) loss of control are involved." He noted that in gamma alcoholism there is (a definite progression from psychological to physical dependence,) and that alpha and beta alcoholism "may develop under given conditions" into gamma alcoholism.[11] Regarding the loss of control over drinking, Jellinek noted that gamma alcoholics might be able to abstain for "shorter or longer periods," but if they begin drinking at any point, they are unable to control the amount of alcohol consumed. This is true despite the mounting harmful consequences that result from their drinking.[12]

Delta alcoholism shares two characteristics with gamma alcoholism: increased tolerance and physical dependence. But instead of loss of control, in delta alcoholism there is an inability to abstain. Delta alcoholics can control the amount they consume on a given occasion, yet they are unable to abstain for even a single day without withdrawal symptoms.[13]

Epsilon alcoholism occurs when excessive drinking occurs in bouts, or a series of episodes.[14]

According to Jellinek, only gamma and delta alcoholism qualify as diseases. His concept of loss of control in gamma alcoholism echoes the classic AA contention: once an alcoholic takes the first drink, he or she is unable to control the amount consumed.

Jellinek carefully qualified his concept of loss of control, pointing out that it developed gradually over several years and did not inevitably follow excessive drinking. He also admitted that drinkers are not deprived of free choice; they can decide whether to take the first drink.[15]

Is alcoholism, then, a self-inflicted disease? In some sense, Jellinek said, it can be viewed this way. Several factors, however, combine to limit the role of choice in alcoholism. First, once the disease process is established, it is no longer within the alcoholic's power to reverse that process without outside help. Second, the disease can develop so gradually that the process is invisible to the drinker.

Third, the disease develops from a specific behavior—drinking—that is considered normal and even desirable by large segments of our society. Few people, for example, raise a glass of beer with the thought *Here's to becoming alcoholic.* People choose to drink—not to become addicted.[16]

Jellinek acknowledged that the disease concept was largely a hypothesis without empirical verification and that he fully expected his original ideas to be modified. And they were. Current views of alcoholism are more complex. We now speak of various alcoholisms with a range of etiologies and characteristics that go beyond Jellinek's fivefold typology.

Shortly after Jellinek's book was published, Timothy Leary and Richard Alpert presaged another shift in the public consciousness. These Harvard psychologists promoted the popular fascination with altered states of consciousness through their controversial experiments with LSD. Later in the decade, Leary's slogan "Turn on, tune in, drop out" appeared on bumper stickers and posters. In addition, sociologist Carlos Casteneda published *The Teachings of Don Juan,* a book about a Mexican sorcerer who used peyote and other drugs to induce altered states of consciousness in his students.[17] That book, followed by others about Don Juan, sold millions of copies.

But drugs were not only used during the 1960s to open the doors of perception. They fulfilled a variety of needs—from controlling stress to transforming physical appearance. Anderson recalls that everything one needed to weather the 1960s was summed up by the "three M's"—Metrical, Miltown, and Mantan. Metrical was a liquid diet for weight loss. Miltown was a minor tranquilizer. And Mantan was a skin application that helped people look tan.[18]

1970-1980

During the 1960s the United States Senate created a special subcommittee on alcoholism and narcotics. It was chaired by Sen. Harold Hughes of Iowa, a recovering alcoholic and former governor of that state. Hughes conducted hearings across the country on alcoholism, his goal being to bring this subject into the national spotlight. He also wanted the federal government to take long-delayed leadership in reforming the treatment of alcoholics and drug addicts.

Hughes's efforts paid off. They culminated in the Comprehensive Alcohol Abuse and Alcoholism Prevention and Treatment Act of 1970 (the Hughes Act). The measure passed unanimously in both houses of Congress. The Hughes Act established national programs for alcoholism education, training, and research, providing funds for all these purposes. To implement the new law, Congress created the National Institute on Alcohol Abuse and Alcoholism (NIAAA).

More progress quickly followed. In 1971, the NIAAA and the National Conference of Commissioners on Uniform State Laws adopted the Uniform Alcoholism and Intoxication Act. This model law decriminalized public drunkenness and mandated treatment as an alternative to incarcerating alcoholics. It said that alcoholism was a public health problem—not one to be solved primarily through use of the criminal justice system. This law, along with the Hughes Act, formed a "Bill of Rights" for alcoholics.

The NIAAA was not the only agency chartered to implement the new policies. The federal government also created the National Institute on Drug Abuse (NIDA) to provide the services for drug addicts that NIAAA was providing for alcoholics. Though NIDA initially focused on heroin addiction, its efforts later expanded to researching and treating other forms of drug addiction. Today NIDA is the largest institution in the world devoted to drug abuse research.[19]

The rush of new federal activity had predictable results: the nation's treatment base grew rapidly. By 1975, NIAAA had either started or supported more than 600 community-based treatment programs. By 1977, there were 2400 programs.

Along with expanded options for treatment came a demand for accountability. Treatment programs now had to meet standards of care and demonstrate their effectiveness. In 1972 the Joint Commission on Accreditation of Hospitals (JCAH) developed voluntary standards for alcoholism treatment programs.[20]

Anderson recalls that this was a valuable, if painful, period for many people in the treatment field:

> Most of us were dedicated to helping sick alcoholics and drug addicts. But we weren't dedicated to fixing responsibility and defining and classifying what we did into units of service, and systematizing this and writing it all down in triplicate—if it isn't written down, it didn't happen. And it took a long time for many of us to get used to this new level of accountability and to begin to realize that it was helpful and appropriate, and to realize that it was and still is the best way to ensure minimum patient care standards.[21]

In 1976, while the push for professional accreditation was going on, the NIAAA published information on one of its most controversial projects: the Rand Report. This concerned a study done by the Rand Corporation with data from NIAAA's Alcoholism Treatment Center Monitoring System. According to some accounts, the Rand Report showed that some recovering alcoholics could return to controlled drinking. Such a conclusion seemed to undercut a basic premise of AA and programs based on the Minnesota Model: that lifelong abstinence from alcohol and other drugs was the goal of treatment.

In reality, the authors of the Rand Report were far more cautious. "The data from this study, and from other similar studies," they wrote, "are simply not adequate to establish, beyond question, the long-term feasibility of normal or "controlled" drinking among alcoholics; nor do the data enable us to identify those specific individuals for whom normal drinking might be appropriate."[22]

In a critique of the Rand Report, J. Clark Laundergan makes these points:[23]

- The findings were affected by sample bias: a disproportionate number of treatment centers included were located in the Southern United States, serving mainly lower-income subjects from ethnic minorities.

- The follow-up data were gathered six months after clients *entered* treatment — not six months after they were *discharged* from treatment. Hence, the study included clients who were still in treatment.

- The study's conclusions were based on a low rate of response at the six-month follow-up date.

- The data came from a mix of settings that used a variety of treatment methods. Thus it is impossible to make any general statement about the effectiveness of those methods.

1980-1990

In the early 1960s there were about 200 treatment programs nationwide. By 1987 there were over 6800.[24] At the same time there were about 73,000 AA groups around the world. And 60 percent of surveyed AA members reported that they had received treatment or counseling for chemical dependency.[25]

In the early 1980s the cycle took a downturn. The early years of the Reagan administration brought substantial budget cuts for health-related agencies in the federal government. In 1981, NIAAA reduced its funding for a number of projects, and treatment centers competed for what funds were left.[26] Here the new president was making good on a campaign promise: to change the federal government's role in solving social problems, largely giving up this initiative to the states.

This movement gained momentum during the Reagan years, when certain attitudes gained political expression. Among these attitudes were skepticism about the sums spent on social services and a focus on individual morality. Implicit in the political metaphors of the Reagan campaign was the Horatio Alger myth, which touted the virtue of self-reliance and the social utility of pulling yourself up by your own bootstraps.

That mythology runs counter to central values of AA and the Minnesota Model: mutual self-help, the admission of personal vulnerability, the need for human relationship, and the necessity of accepting outside help to begin recovery. The conservative political agenda of the 1980s made it possible to revive old ideas about alcoholics and addicts—that they are weak-willed louts who simply lack the personal moral discipline to better themselves.

The trend has continued and taken new turns. President George Bush's budget request for 1992 included nearly $8 billion for a "war on drugs." Included here were funds for law enforcement efforts to capture and prosecute drug dealers. That left only $1.655 billion for treatment and $1.515 billion for education and prevention. [27]

The results of the war on drugs are mixed. There is little evidence that interdiction efforts have reduced the supply of cocaine, marijuana, and other illicit drugs. Moreover, the war ignores our two largest drug problems—alcohol and nicotine.

The other major shift in American health care during the 1980s was cost containment. Business owners and federal agencies, who were paying the bulk of the nation's health care bills, began revolting against the amount of money they were spending. With health care insurance doubling in cost every four years, it became apparent that the situation was out of control. Along with the fees for other kinds of health care, costs for chemical dependency came under scrutiny.

Managed care soon became a major player on the scene. *Managed care* is an umbrella term that includes any organized effort to contain health care costs. Such efforts evolved from the belief that health dollars were being wasted on unnecessary and overpriced treatment.

Health maintenance organizations (HMOs) and preferred provider organizations (PPOs) are examples of managed care. Both are groups of health care providers who contract to provide services for a fixed, sometimes discounted, fee.

Managed care also includes private companies hired by an insurance company or self-insured business. These companies seek to reduce health care costs for their clients by using several methods. One is precertification; that is, making sure that patients meet certain requirements for admission to a treatment program. Another is concurrent review, which means continuously monitoring a patient's progress in treatment. Third are outcome studies that establish the cost-effectiveness of a given treatment.

All of this directly affects Minnesota Model programs. One immediate result of managed care was a shift in the kind of treatment insurers were willing to pay for: a move from inpatient care to less expensive outpatient care.

Another result is that treatment options are shrinking. Harold Swift, former vice chairman of public policy for Hazelden, noted in 1992 that "treatment programs have a vacancy rate of about 50 percent nationwide and an estimated 200 inpatient treatment programs across the country have closed during the last two years alone."[28] Even Hazelden, which had a waiting list for years, was at 80 percent occupancy during early 1993.[29]

At the same time, the number of people who need treatment remains constant or is growing. Only a fraction of adult alcoholics are getting help for drinking problems; this includes *any* kind of help, not just AA or Minnesota Model treatment.

The current system of health care funding creates an irony: Minnesota Model treatment programs are becoming increasingly inaccessible—even to people in Minnesota! This is true even though chemical dependency treatment is a mandated benefit. Yet thousands of people in Minnesota receive health care through HMOs, which often deny or restrict coverage for chemical dependency treatment. Their reason? Such services are often deemed not "medically necessary."

What's involved here is a discrepancy between the rehabilitation model and the traditional medical model. For example, Hazelden requires that people admitted to its treatment program meet certain requirements: they have to be intellectually alert, ambulatory, and well enough to do routine self-care. These are basic features of the rehabilitation model. But managed care companies who don't understand the concept of rehabilitation can easily conclude that such patients are not appropriate candidates for inpatient care because they are not "sick" enough.

Add to this the growing number of employers who are self-insured. These companies often fall under different regulations than other employers, and they are not required to provide similar levels of coverage for chemical dependency.

When it came to the relationship between managed care firms and treatment providers, the 1980s were a decade of contention. There was overreaction on all sides. In trying to contain costs, some businesses, insurance companies, and government agencies turned to outpatient programs as their panacea. Other programs reached for the other extreme, claiming that nearly every alcoholic or addict needs inpatient treatment. Along with this came some basic confusion about the Minnesota Model—*the idea that it can only be delivered in a residential setting.*

The rancor can soften if we become client-centered again. Some patients require inpatient treatment for chemical dependency. Others will do well in outpatient programs. Still others need a variety of stops on the continuum of care, some less costly than others.

Summing Up

When Nelson Bradley first unlocked the ward doors at Willmar State Hospital, there was little recognition of the need to treat alcoholics in any comprehensive way. Since then, chemical dependency treatment has made inroads into the "big leagues." For several decades it gained increasing acceptance among mainstream health care providers. Treatment programs started to be licensed in many states and accredited by bodies such as the JCAH. Alcoholism and drug addiction counselors were certified, and health insurers offered coverage for chemical dependency treatment.

The Minnesota Model evolved too, and has been modified in some significant ways since 1950. Many of these modifications relate to services that extend the continuum of care: information, evaluation, and referral centers; extended residential care; intermediate residential care, such as halfway houses; aftercare programs; and family programs. In addition, the model is now being extended to people who have been chronically underserved when it comes to chemical dependency treatment: older adults, adolescents, people with disabilities, people of color, and gays and lesbians.

At the same time, we face entrenched attitudes that hinder treatment. "Alcohol is cheap, accessible, familiar, and legal," notes Harold Swift. "We don't think of it as a drug. Our ambivalence about alcohol allows us to sanction its use while rejecting its victims."[30] And Harold Hughes, who now heads SOAR, the Society of Americans for Recovery, notes how widely chemical dependency is still ignored:

> Controlling alcoholism and other drug dependence would probably be the greatest contributing factor to slowing the spread of AIDS in the Unites States, yet no one talks about it. Chemical dependency is a major contributor to cancer and heart disease, yet little is said about it. We wage major debates over the issue of abortion, yet rarely does anyone link the thousands of unwanted pregnancies to alcohol and other drugs. Fetal alcohol syndrome is one of the top three known causes of birth defects with accompanying mental retardation, but it doesn't get the attention it deserves.[31]

What's more, recovering people still face waves of discrimination. They find it hard to secure life, health, and disability insurance; they struggle with whether to reveal their treatment history to prospective employers and landlords; and they may be denied federal benefits for education and housing even if they've been sober for years.

In some ways, the Minnesota Model has suffered from its own success. The pioneers of this grass-roots social movement decided that chemical dependency treatment ought to become part of the medical system. Treatment providers worked hard to shape public policy, pass laws such as the Hughes Act, change attitudes in the medical community, and become part of mainstream health care. Underlying it all was a mission to bring treatment to everyone who needed it.

The question was how to make treatment widely available, and that involved money. Who would pay for chemical dependency treatment? Individuals could pay their own way, the government could pay, or employers could pay, most often through health insurance. Lacking other options, the pioneers of the Minnesota Model opted for payment through health insurance.

Yet the Minnesota Model, as a social movement, has never wholly succeeded. Rehabilitation care, which underlies the model, is often not understood by those steeped in the practice of acute medical care. Rehabilitation emphasizes education and calls for patients to assume responsibility for their own recovery. This is diametrically opposed to the traditional doctor-patient relationship. In short, decisions about treatment services are often made by people completely uninformed about the nature of chemical dependency.

Moreover, treatment is now more driven by financial issues than ever before. And traditional types of cost containment are often at odds with rehabilitation care. Minnesota Model programs simply don't provide the short-term acute care that can be rendered less costly through shorter length of stays.

Managed care companies and insurers can feel real frustration when it comes to sorting out the facts about chemical dependency treatment. Part of the reason is that treatment providers have not always carefully explained what they do or taken the time to demonstrate their outcomes.

As a result, the Minnesota Model has come under fire. The next chapter examines ideas from some of the model's major critics.

CHAPTER FIVE

Critics and Criticism

The Minnesota Model has received its share of criticism. Many of the critics speak not to the model specifically but to some of the model's primary tenets. Among these are the spiritual program of AA and the disease concept of chemical dependency. Other criticisms center on the effectiveness of treatment—not only of Minnesota Model programs but of *any* treatment program. Here the underlying question is, Does treatment really make a difference, and how do we find that out?

This chapter presents an overview of ideas from six prominent critics. There are, of course, others who have pointed out shortcomings in the kind of treatment offered by the Minnesota Model. Yet if we examine the ideas of these six people and organizations, we emerge with a representative cross-section of critical reaction to the Minnesota Model.

SECULAR ORGANIZATIONS FOR SOBRIETY

James Christopher is the founder of Secular Organizations for Sobriety (SOS) and the author of *How To Stay Sober: Recovery Without Religion.* When surveying current methods of treating chemical dependency, Christopher is most disturbed by the spiritual program of AA.

"AA insists that its programs and precepts are 'spiritual,' not religious," Christopher writes. "But there are a lot people who cannot

73

relate to AA's version of spirituality, or who don't consider themselves religious or 'spiritual' at all. They have a hard time believing that faith in the supernatural is a prerequisite for sobriety."[1]

Christopher does acknowledge that AA is a powerful option for some people. He maintains, however, that many members eventually drift away from AA. Furthermore, the program reaches only a minority of alcoholics in the first place.

Recovery programs of any type tend to enter people's lives when they are most vulnerable, Christopher notes. He argues for a recovery program that does not demand people sacrifice their intellectual integrity or compromise their individuality. Christopher agrees that people in recovery need "emotional inspiration," but he sees AA as advocating a return to a more primitive state of mind. In making this argument, he relies on a book titled *The Origins of Consciousness in the Breakdown of the Bicameral Mind*. The author, Julian Jaynes, argues that in prehistoric times, messages from the right hemisphere of the human brain were believed to be the commanding voices of the gods. When AA speaks of "conscious contact" with a Higher Power, says Christopher, it is calling for a regression to this type of ancient, superstitious thinking.[2]

Christopher also argues that AA members can be rigid, dogmatic, and intolerant of other approaches to recovery. He gives a personal example:

> Not long ago, I traveled to meet a man whose work in the field of alcoholism I greatly admired. The meeting, unfortunately, did not go well. Together with an openly hostile colleague, he cornered me in a heated grill-fest over coffee. I'd expected civility and a stimulating exchange of ideas. Astonishingly, and insultingly, both of them denied my sobriety, not to mention the sobriety of legions of others [who] recovered without religion.
>
> One becomes used to this kind of encounter: "How dare you be sober 'n' happy without my Lord . . . or my one-hand clapping?" I dare to be, and I am.[3]

The attitude Christopher says he encountered in AA was, Do as I say or else you'll lose your sobriety. In response, he felt threatened.

The following ideas are implicit in AA, states Christopher:[4]

- Belief in a Higher Power is a necessity for staying sober.

- Recovering people will drink again if they fail to "work" the Steps.

- Recovering people will drink again if they fail to attend many AA meetings.

- If recovering people fail to "carry the message," they will drink again.

- If they leave AA, recovering people will drink again.

Each of these claims, says Christopher, is untrue.

Christopher wants us to remember that people who remain sober do not need to be religious. Rather, they remain sober because they do not drink. Indeed, they do not even *consider* drinking. These people see their sobriety as an issue separate from every other in their lives. No matter what happens with their relationships, their finances, their jobs, or their moods, recovering people take one thing as a given: they simply cannot use alcohol.

Unlike religious approaches to sobriety, writes Christopher, SOS does not offer a "magic, quick fix." In SOS, members get to keep their individuality and their integrity. In addition, "you need not check your mind at the door upon entering."[5]

Christopher offers a model of dependency—the "cycle of addiction," as he calls it. There are three factors at work here. First is a chemical *need* for alcohol existing at the cellular level. Second is a learned *habit* (chronic drinking). Third is the alcoholic's *denial* that either the need or the habit exists.

Contrast with this the cycle of sobriety. Here recovering people acknowledge daily that they are alcoholics or addicts. They accept that they cannot use alcohol or any other any mind-altering drug—no matter how negative their moods become. Finally, they view sobriety as the first priority in their lives and an issue separate from every other. The three crucial elements of sobriety, then, are daily *acknowledgment* of addiction, daily *acceptance* of the need for abstinence, and daily *prioritization* of sobriety as a separate issue.[6]

Viewing sobriety as a separate issue means recovering people can feel any emotional state—no matter how pleasant or unpleasant—without having to feel they are "dry drunks" or about to relapse. It also means that people of any religious persuasion—or none at all—any profession, any political party, or any economic station are welcome in SOS.

RATIONAL RECOVERY SYSTEMS

Jack Trimpey founded Rational Recovery Systems (RRS), a program based on the Rational-Emotive Therapy (RET) of psychologist Albert Ellis. Trimpey has also written a basic RRS text titled *The Small Book.*

Like James Christopher, Trimpey acknowledges the value of AA for many people. "I have a fundamental respect for Alcoholics Anonymous," he states. "When I reached out for help with my own alcohol dependence, it was there—a fellowship of concerned human beings helping themselves by helping others. I have been to many of their meetings and I learned some important information about alcohol dependence."[7]

Even so, says Trimpey, programs based on the Twelve Steps have dominated the treatment field for too long. Trimpey objects to the way that AA has been sold to the public. He agrees that in its simple communal form, AA is wonderful. But today, Trimpey asserts, AA is enforced as *the* treatment of choice by powerful institutions— including the military, the courts, and health care providers. This lack of choice is one of his main quarrels with AA. He argues that democracy demands alcoholics have more than one recovery program to choose from. Trimpey's mentor, Albert Ellis, agrees in his introduction to *The Small Book*:

> RRS, moreover, is the most effective way to establish a two-party system for helping alcoholics. AA definitely has its place in this system and I have referred literally hundreds of people to it during the last half-century, many of whom have been helped to stay off booze. But democracy requires at least two influential parties, not one; and RRS provides a fine meeting ground for great numbers of people who want nothing to do with any kind of Higher Power and who want (with the use of RET) to achieve and maintain sobriety.[8]

Trimpey agrees with some of the basic tenets of AA, including the need for recovering people to abstain from alcohol and other drugs for a lifetime. Still, he argues, we need an alternative to AA — one that is more rational.

Trimpey also disagrees with the religious beliefs he claims are part of the AA agenda. He notes that the spiritual healing advocated by AA is simply unworkable for millions of people who want nothing to do with belief in God or even the more neutral term, *higher power*.

For Trimpey, Rational Recovery boils down to two directives: First, decide to quit drinking for good. Second, do it! All the principles and practices explained in *The Small Book* exist merely to help people sustain this fundamental decision and choice of action.[9]

The Small Book has elicited some emotional reactions. A reviewer for the *Boston Globe* labeled the book an "angry manifesto." The mere existence of an alternative to AA, he notes, is inherently threatening to some people. One woman who attended a presentation by Trimpey compared him to Muammar Qaddafi.[10]

Trimpey divides humanity into those who believe and those who think. Admittedly, he writes, this is an oversimplification: people do both. Yet individuals tend to cluster around one of those two poles: thinking or feeling. Furthermore, AA is not "wrong"; rather, it is wrong for people who gravitate primarily toward thinking.

It is fitting, then, that Trimpey views alcoholism primarily as a way of thinking. The alcoholic is practicing a certain philosophy of life. Unfortunately for the alcoholic, that philosophy is largely irrational.

Trimpey sums up some of the irrational beliefs that he believes fuel alcoholism:[11]

- "I am powerless over my alcoholic cravings, and therefore not responsible for what I put in my mouth. . . ." The more rational idea is that we can voluntarily control the motion of our arms, hands, and facial muscles.

- "In order to feel like a worthwhile person, I must stop drinking. . . ." The more rational idea is that the very decision to stop drinking reinforces the fact that we are worthwhile.

- "My painful emotions and alcoholic cravings are intolerable, and therefore must be controlled by drinking alcohol. . . ." In reality, emotional discomfort is inevitable—a normal part of becoming sober.

- "I have little control over my feelings and emotions, which are somehow forced upon me by certain persons or by external events. . . ." Actually, states Trimpey, we feel the way we think. And because we can choose to redirect our thoughts, we have enormous control over our feelings.

Following the lead of Rational-Emotive Therapy, Trimpey believes our moods are largely the product of our thoughts. With practice, we can direct our thinking, moderate our emotions, and produce lasting change in our behavior.

WOMEN FOR SOBRIETY

Jean Kirkpatrick is another recovering person who values AA yet sees a fundamental limitation in the Twelve Step program: AA, founded and still dominated by men, falls short of affirming the unique experience of female addicts and alcoholics.

Kirkpatrick says AA came into being when it was believed that few women had drinking problems. In addition, treatment programs still lag behind in providing services geared to the special needs of women. Women face greater obstacles in recovering from alcoholism, yet have the least amount of help available.[12]

Despite the organization's effectiveness, Kirkpatrick has another problem with AA. "Alcoholics Anonymous has been the single most successful help available to alcoholics for 40 years," she notes. "There is no one that could challenge this. . . . But despite its great successes, only 6 to 10 percent of all alcoholics ever get to AA and only 3.5 to 5 percent of all women alcoholics ever do."[13]

Kirkpatrick contrasts the Twelve Steps of AA with thirteen "statements of acceptance" that form the basis of Women for Sobriety. Examples of those statements are "The past is gone forever," "I am what I think," "I am a competent woman and have much to give others," and "I am responsible for myself and my sisters."[14]

Like AA, Women for Sobriety is a network of self-help groups that meet as often as they choose. And like the Twelve Steps, the statements of acceptance place heavy emphasis on spiritual growth.

"The Women for Sobriety program is an affirmation of the value and worth of each woman," Kirkpatrick writes. "It is a program that leads each woman to asserting her belief in self, a program that leads her to seeing herself in a positive and self-confident image."[15]

FINGARETTE AND THE "HEAVY DRINKING" HYPOTHESIS

Herbert Fingarette is the author of *Heavy Drinking: The Myth of Alcoholism as a Disease.* He believes the disease concept promoted by AA and the Minnesota Model is a fallacy.

More specifically, Fingarette disagrees with Jellinek's description of loss of control as it occurs in alcoholic drinking. "One drink, one drunk," the old saying by some AA members, is simply naive folk-lore, states Fingarette:

> According to this disease concept, alcoholism progresses stage by stage in a regular, fairly standard course that does not respect a person's individual characteristics. . . . Most crucially: those affected by the disease *inevitably* progress to uncontrolled drinking because the disease produces a distinctive disability—"loss of control," a loss of "the power of choice in the matter of drinking."[16]

These assertions are a hindrance, not a help, in treating alcoholism, argues Fingarette. He criticizes Jellinek's explanation of the disease concept, since it was originally based on data from only ninety-eight male members of AA. In addition, he points out, the questionnaire used to elicit that data was designed and distributed by AA. He argues that later surveys of heavy drinkers' behavior contradict the stages explained by Jellinek, and that even Jellinek acknowledged the tentative nature of his ideas along with the lack of empirical evidence. Fingarette claims that the classic description of alcoholism as a "disease with a unique sequence of stages and a regular pattern of symptoms" has failed to win general acceptance in the scientific community.[17]

For Fingarette the idea of alcoholic craving rests on a "semantic trick" that involves a circular definition: some people drink excessively because they crave alcohol; but when they fail to drink excessively, we simply say that they were not experiencing craving. Craving thus fails as an explanation of excessive drinking: "The consensus in the research literature is that even in their normal, everyday settings, chronic heavy drinkers often moderate their drinking or abstain voluntarily, the choice depending on their perceptions of the costs and benefits."[18]

Fingarette also disputes evidence for the biological basis of alcoholism. He claims heredity is only one factor in the etiology of alcoholism, and even then it only applies in a minority of cases.[19] Even if we could establish a difference in the metabolism of alcoholics and nonalcoholics, he argues, it would not account for drinking behaviors. Instead, it would only account for the heavy drinker's unique experience of intoxication.[20] Finally, a significant number of people labeled as alcoholics do not develop the signs of physiological dependence on alcohol: tolerance and withdrawal symptoms.[21]

"Research today has shown that no one causal formula explains why people become heavy drinkers," adds Fingarette. "Indeed, the attempt to find a single catchall 'cause' of a single 'disease' has repeatedly led researchers astray."[22] He believes that what we take as self-evident truths about alcohol are actually beliefs that vary widely across cultures.

Fingarette stops short of saying that there has been a conspiracy to suppress evidence that contradicts the classic disease concept. But this "scientifically discredited" concept, he writes, has been promoted by powerful political and economic institutions, including the health care industry. For treatment programs to give up the disease concept would undermine their financial survival. Hence, claims Fingarette, treatment providers have a financial interest in persuading governmental agencies, health insurers, and clients that alcoholism is a disease.[23] Similarly, the economics of research funding helps promote the disease concept: "The royal road to public support and funding for research in contemporary American political life is the claim that the work bears on public health and the conquest of disease."[24]

The disease concept even serves the self-interest of liquor companies, notes Fingarette. Because only a small percentage of the population is at risk for acquiring the disease of alcoholism, these companies can claim that the vast majority of consumers and potential consumers are not at risk for experiencing drinking problems. The disease concept is surely more palatable to the liquor industry than the prescriptions of the temperance movement and Prohibition. After all, the latter criminalized the entire liquor industry.[25]

Most people succumb to the disease concept, claims Fingarette, because they dearly hope for a medical miracle that will "cure" the disease of alcoholism. This leads to their uncritical acceptance of treatment programs. "None of these programs has ever been demonstrated to achieve improvements superior to any other type of help," writes Fingarette.[26] Indeed, the very word *treatment* seems a misnomer. The current consensus in the research community, according to Fingarette, is that claims for the effectiveness of disease-oriented treatment are unfounded.

Fingarette offers "heavy drinking" as a more accurate hypothesis than the concept of alcoholism. Simply put, heavy drinkers are people for whom drinking has become a "central activity" in life. For these people, says Fingarette, drinking assumes the importance that a career does for others. Heavy drinkers are diverse, showing little in common except these things: they drink a lot, they tend to have more problems than nondrinkers and moderate drinkers, and they do not consistently manage their drinking.[27]

The notion of drinking as a central activity has a crucial implication. Heavy drinkers must do more than stop drinking—they must reconstruct their entire way of life. What's more, personal responsibility plays a major role in this effort.

PEELE DECRIES THE "DISEASING OF AMERICA"

In *The Diseasing of America: Addiction Treatment Out of Control*, Stanton Peele argues against three basic premises that widely pervade treatment programs:[28]

- Addiction is an autonomous drive that fuels all choices.
- Addiction is progressive and irreversible. An addict's condition will inevitably worsen unless he or she gets medical treatment or joins a Twelve Step group.
- People cannot control their addictive behavior.

Contrary to these claims, writes Peele, "people are *active agents* in—not passive victims of—their addictions."[29] And he sums up his thesis with the claim that "we will never, ever *treat* away drug abuse, alcoholism, and the host of other behaviors that are now called addictive disease."[30]

Like Fingarette, Peele focuses on the disease concept. He begins his criticism by posing a simple question: What, after all, *is* a disease? Our answers to this question have run through three generations. At first the term *disease* applied only to physical ailments such as tuberculosis or cancer. Later the term included mental disorders. Only recently has the term embraced alcohol and other drug addictions.

In accepting this final extension of the definition, says Peele, we have stretched the concept of disease beyond its reasonable limits. Such thinking implies that we can treat *any* kind of undesirable behavior— from compulsive sexual activity to procrastination—as a disease.

The disease concept has a host of other negative consequences, writes Peele. Among them are the following:[31]

- Categorizing certain behaviors as addictive disease fails to accomplish the central goal of the disease concept: encouraging people to seek medical treatment.

- Even if people do enter treatment, the disease concept again proves ineffective. Studies indicate that treated and untreated people fare about the same in learning to overcome addictive behaviors.

- Because the disease concept is so widely accepted, people are often coerced into treatment as an alternative to jail or loss of a job. Such actions resemble totalitarianism.

- Organizations and treatment facilities that promote the disease concept use techniques that resemble brainwashing. People who disagree with their disease diagnosis are told they are in denial, and that this is further evidence of their sickness.

- The disease concept undermines the idea of personal and moral responsibility. By labeling certain behaviors as diseases, we merely end up defending self-indulgent behavior.

- The disease concept deprives us of the chance to grow. It denies us the opportunity to accept our weaknesses and imperfections as part of the process of learning through life experience: "Less of our personal selves, our relationships with our children, and our private views of life remains our own, while normal joy and pain are denied us through being defined as clinical syndromes."

Peele confesses that *The Diseasing of America* was rejected by several publishers who thought his message lacked compassion for people with addictions. In reality, he argues, it shows a true lack of compassion to tell someone who drinks in response to life stress that he or she is an alcoholic who can never drink again. [32]

KAMINER: "CHANCES ARE YOU'RE CODEPENDENT, TOO"

In her book *I'm Dysfunctional, You're Dysfunctional: The Recovery Movement and Other Self-Help Fashions*, Wendy Kaminer takes a critical look at Twelve Step groups as an aspect of popular culture.

Kaminer begins by admitting that many thoughtful people are helped by the Steps. Her indictment of the recovery *movement* is not meant to be an indictment of recovering *people*. Kaminer also states that she personally knows people who recovered through AA. Furthermore, her knowledge of the Twelve Steps is that of an outsider, not a member of the movement. [33] Thus she has neither the desire nor the capacity to refute accounts of recovery based on the Steps.

Even so, writes Kaminer, "Twelve-step groups depress me—so many people talking about such relatively trivial problems with such seriousness, in the same nonsensical jargon." [34] For her the recovery movement's success, especially when it drifts to the topic of codependency, can be explained by two facts of human nature: people enjoy talking about themselves and venting anger about their parents. "You don't have to be in denial to doubt that truths like these will set us free," Kaminer notes. [35]

Twelve Step groups also succeed because they mirror other aspects of our culture. They're like 7-Eleven stores, says Kaminer: you can enter one anywhere in the country and feel at home. And sometimes attending one of these groups is a bit like watching MTV; you expose yourself to a continuous succession of disconnected stories. [36]

One of Kaminer's main problems with the recovery movement is that it promotes passivity and a search for simple absolutes. [37] She's also concerned about prescribing techniques that are universally applicable as a substitute for individual self-knowledge. Self-help experts, notes Kaminer, deny believing in quick fixes but go ahead and deliver them anyway.

It's essential for us to recognize the true nature of Twelve Step groups, says Kaminer: "Demanding self-surrender, the recovery movement is essentially religious, not psychotherapeutic, and most closely resembles 19th-century revivalism, with a little Christian Science thrown in."[38] Interestingly enough, Kaminer does not accuse the recovery movement of being a cult, saying it is far too flexible and disorganized for that. Still, she fears the power of the recovery movement to render people self-absorbed and apolitical:

> The self-help tradition has always been covertly authoritarian and conformist, relying as it does on the mystique of expertise, encouraging people to look outside themselves for standardized instructions on how to be, teaching us that different people with different problems can easily be saved by the same techniques. It is anathema to independent thought. [39]

Summing Up

Many of the critics quoted in this chapter still agree with key points of the Minnesota Model. For example, the Secular Organization for Sobriety, Rational Recovery Systems, and Women for Sobriety all acknowledge the power of AA for many people. These movements also support lifelong abstinence. And Christopher's account of his meeting with some overzealous members of AA reminds us that we must return to the spirit of the Big Book, which urges AA members to practice tolerance and avoid holding out the Twelve Steps as an exclusive path to recovery.

Advocates of the Minnesota Model often share this attitude of live and let live. A dogmatic attachment to the model violates the methods used by its earliest developers—guesses, trial and error, and creative hunches. Like the Twelve Steps of AA, the Minnesota Model was born of provisional experiments not intended to be panaceas, final solutions, or quick fixes.

At the same time, there is a basic axiom of intellectual etiquette: before criticizing an opposing point of view, take pains to understand it. In that spirit, the next chapter offers further clarification about three widely misunderstood aspects of the Minnesota Model.

Chapter Six

Three Points About
The Minnesota Model

Bill W. was fond of reminding people that AA was never intended to be the solution to alcoholism. Confronted by other approaches to recovery that could demonstrate success, Bill no doubt would have admonished them to "go for it." Late in his life, Bill himself experimented with LSD and massive doses of vitamins, which he thought had the potential to enhance or surpass the significance of AA.

The primary purpose of this book is to promote an accurate understanding the Minnesota Model—not to offer a point-by-point response to its critics. Yet we can dispel some misunderstandings that surround the model. Most of them cluster around three topics:

- The spirituality of AA
- The claim that chemical dependency is a disease
- The effectiveness of treatment programs based on the model

Understanding Twelve Step Spirituality

It's understandable that some newcomers to AA react with dismay at all the "God talk" in the Twelve Steps. Many early AA members were religious in a traditional sense, and their ideas about a Higher Power had much in common with orthodox Christian conceptions of God.

But to say that alcoholism and drug addiction have a spiritual dimension does not banish it to a mysterious, otherwordly realm that resists all attempts at scientific understanding. *Any* disease has a spiritual dimension. Diabetes, coronary artery disease, multiple sclerosis, cancer—all these conditions confront us with our limitations, our mortality. They bring questions about the meaning and purpose of human life to the foreground.

What's more, AA is grounded in spirituality, not organized religion. As a program of action, it emphasizes *doing* over believing. The Steps endure not because they recommend a doctrine, but because they recommend a set of *practices.* AA members who "carry the message" to other alcoholics are directed by the Big Book not to preach religion but simply to share their stories. The task of recovering people is to tell what they were like when they were practicing addicts, and to explain how their lives have changed since achieving sobriety. These individual stories promote identification of a common experience. When this process achieves its purpose, the practicing alcoholic is able to say, *Yes, that's the way it is for me, too, right now. There must be something about this AA program.*

Bill W. and the earliest members of AA also saw the wisdom in respecting individual differences. This was true from the beginning of the movement, embodied in a question posed by Bill's former drinking buddy, Ebby T.: "Why don't you just choose your own conception of God?" Nothing more than this, notes the Big Book, is required to get started.

As AA historian Ernest Kurtz notes, AA thrives on pluralism. Where else but at a Twelve Step meeting can you find an atheist, an agnostic, a fundamentalist Christian, and even a Zen Buddhist engaged in a common purpose—the effort to stay sober for the next twenty-four hours? An atheist member of AA summed it up well: "People use the word *spiritual* in ways that define themselves. I think it means the ability to get outside one's own immediate concerns to perform an altruistic act."[1]

UNDERSTANDING THE DISEASE CONCEPT

Arguments against the disease concept often start from a false premise. They are based on the mistaken belief that *disease* has a specific, tightly defined, scientifically based meaning. But no such consensus exists on the meaning of the term *disease*—or of the word *health*, for that matter. Even Bill W. was wary of using the term *disease* when referring to alcoholism. He knew it might stir up public controversy. Consequently, Bill often used the terms *malady* and *illness* to describe alcoholism.[2]

With these ideas in mind, here are some reasons for accepting the disease concept.

Chemical Dependency Mirrors Other Diseases

Chemical dependency overlaps in many respects with other conditions we call diseases. George Vaillant makes this point in his influential book, *The Natural History of Alcoholism: Causes, Common Patterns, and Paths to Recovery*. Vaillant writes that we need to satisfy four criteria before including a condition within the disease concept:[3]

- The factors causing the disorder must be "independent of social deviance"—that is, of immoral or illegal behavior.
- A diagnosis of disease should offer "shorthand information" about the signs, symptoms, and possible course of the condition.
- The diagnosis should be valid across cultures.
- The diagnosis should suggest an appropriate medical response.

Judged against these four criteria, alcoholism passes with flying colors. It affects people of every socioeconomic class, ethnic group, and nation. It affects not only people on the margins of society, but also respected members of the community with solid family and professional lives. The term *alcoholism* also gives a meaningful description of the symptoms we can expect to see (including physical dependence), and of the desired treatment (including medically supervised detoxification).

Other people who object to the disease concept claim that it's more accurate to describe alcoholism as a behavioral disorder than a disease. According to these critics, this makes alcoholism treatment the stepchild of psychology, not medical science. If we start labeling any undesirable behavior a disease, then we render the term meaningless. Vaillant replies that alcoholism is unique because it involves a need for acute medical care, including detoxification.

The disease concept "works" even if we adopt criteria that are less stringent than Vaillant's. We can, for example, provisionally define *disease* as a condition that has physical effects and a biological basis, and that functions as an involuntary disability. Alcoholism and drug addiction pass these tests too.

First, let's consider the physical effects. The Sixth Special Report to the U.S. Congress on Alcohol and Health mentions these figures: from 20 to 40 percent of all hospital beds are occupied by people with complications resulting from alcohol abuse or alcoholism. Long-term alcoholism can damage almost every organ system in the body and cause death. [4]

Second is the biological basis of alcoholism and other drug addiction. Evidence for this comes from the signs and symptoms of alcohol withdrawal. These include tremors, sweating, increased heart rate, hyperactive reflexes, nausea, and vomiting. Beyond these, some people report nightmares and hallucinations, even an alcoholic epilepsy that involves grand mal seizures. Delirium tremens (d.t.'s) is a severe form of alcohol withdrawal—one that can be fatal.

Besides withdrawal syndrome, there is another biological sign for addiction: increased tolerance. The latter means that the drinker must consume increasingly more alcohol to produce the desired physical and emotional effects. Some alcoholics even develop tolerance to toxic chemicals such as methanol, and can drink them in amounts that would kill nonalcoholics.

Moreover, there's evidence that alcoholism runs in families. Heredity is not the only factor, but it increases a person's risk for developing the condition. To date the strongest predictor of alcoholism in any given individual is still a family history of alcoholism. In addition, we don't have to understand the biological basis of a condition before we call it a disease. An example is diabetes, which existed long before we understood the role of insulin deficiency in this disease.

A third facet of the disease concept is the notion of involuntary disability, or the constricting effect of the disease. That means people with a disease find that their responses are less flexible. Their behavior may become rigid, stereotyped, and repetitive. Chemically dependent people, who continue to use alcohol or other drugs despite the mounting and devastating consequences, are a prime example. In contrast, healthy people are flexible. When survival requires them to change their behavior, they can do so.

Daniel Anderson explains it this way:

> A disease is involuntary: We don't choose cancer, pneumonia, or diabetes. This is true even with illness caused by "lifestyle." The person who lights up a cigarette doesn't say, "Well, here's to lung cancer!" The behavior has gone beyond willfull misconduct. It's more than a bad habit. It's beyond control.[5]

More evidence for the disease concept of chemical dependency comes from the failed history of treating the condition as if it were a moral failure; that is, to treat chemically dependent people as criminals.

There's a problem with this option: it's already been tried and abandoned. Until the Comprehensive Alcohol Abuse and Alcoholism Prevention, Treatment and Rehabilitation Act of 1970, public drunkenness in the United States was treated largely as a criminal problem. This act, in effect, admitted that the criminal justice solution was a failure. It also mandated treatment for alcoholics instead of prison.

Three Points About The Minnesota Model

The Disease Concept Is Therapeutically Useful

There are shades of meaning within the disease concept. One division is between those who insist that chemical dependency is a diagnosable medical entity on par with any "real" disease. Other supporters of the disease concept point primarily to the practical benefits of the concept. To them, treating chemical dependency *as if it were a disease* yields distinct therapeutic advantages.

Remember that the Minnesota Model is both pragmatic and provisional. Its acceptance of the disease concept comes in that spirit. J. Clark Laundergan makes this point in defining the model: "It should not be concluded, however, that the disease concept is assumed to be either correct or incorrect in the Hazelden conceptualization of alcoholism, but rather that it is a convenient and necessary metaphor."[6]

Among the therapeutic benefits of the disease concept are these:

- When alcoholism is viewed as a disease, funding for researching the condition is mobilized. Jack H. Mendelson and Nancy K. Mello, authors of *Alcohol Use and Abuse in America*, underscore this point:

  > Once resources became available, scientists began to study alcoholism as a biomedical disorder, and what might be justifiably called the dark ages of alcoholism came to an end. In very practical terms, that's what it means to be designated as a bona fide disease instead of a moral aberration.[7]

- Accepting the disease concept can reduce guilt on the part of the chemically dependent person and persuade that person to enter treatment.

- The disease concept helps promote treatment over punishment, granting alcoholics and addicts the same civil rights accorded to other people with chronic illnesses and disabilities.

We can use the disease concept as powerful support for treatment—even if we cannot agree on a precise definition of *disease* or validate the concept through controlled research. Treating chemical dependency *as if it were a disease* leads to breakthroughs in recovery that can help thousands of people begin a life that restores them to sanity.

The Disease Concept Promotes Abstinence

The disease concept is also useful because it emphasizes the value of lifelong abstinence for the recovering person. This is crucial in light of people such as Herbert Fingarette, who espouse "controlled drinking" as a possible goal for people in treatment.

Laundergan points out several difficulties with studies of controlled drinking. One is reaching agreement on precisely what "controlled" or "normal" drinking means for any given person. Second, such studies have an ambiguous time frame and do not indicate how long a person can continue to drink and remain free of harmful consequences. Third, the studies often place alcohol *abusers* in the same group with people who are truly *addicted* to alcohol. Abusers, even though they drink excessively, can choose to abstain when the consequences become grave enough. Addicts cannot.[8]

If we accept the idea that controlled drinking is possible for alcoholics, we still lack an effective method for achieving this goal. All that the research indicates is this: controlled drinking may *theoretically* be possible for a small percentage of drinkers. But we presently have no reliable way to determine whether an individual drinker falls into that category.

Minnesota Model treatment calls for lifelong abstinence from mind-altering chemicals. The reason is not to deny people pleasure. Abstinence is simply the safest choice. The practical experience of recovering people and clinical research reveal the same thing: attempts at controlled drinking or drug use pose many dangers. Recovering people who attempt controlled drinking risk illness, injury, death, and a return to the negative consequences they formerly experienced while drinking.

Debates about controlled drinking often miss the point made by both AA and the Minnesota Model: *alcoholics and other drug addicts have* been *unable to achieve sustained sobriety through their own unaided efforts.* This fact transcends the myopic debate about exactly how many drinks recovering alcoholics can take before they "lose control."

The Disease Concept Promotes Personal Responsibility

If we accept the disease concept, say critics, then forget about holding addicts and alcoholics accountable for their behavior. Chemically dependent people have at their disposal a ready-made and universal defense: *I can't help doing what I do. I'm sick.*

Nothing could be further from the truth. In Minnesota Model treatment, much of an individual's recovery comes about as a result of his or her own decisions and actions. Both choice and personal responsibility for recovery are affirmed. Likewise, personal responsibility is at the core of AA's Twelve Steps. The term *powerlessness* as used in Step One refers only to a person's loss of ability to use mind-altering chemicals safely. Even so, the same person has the power to begin a program of recovery if he or she chooses.

Here we regard chemical dependency in the same light as other conditions that are deeply influenced by personal choice. Cancer, coronary artery disease, and diabetes are readily accepted as diseases, even though lifestyle factors—such as diet, exercise, and smoking—may play a role in the onset of these conditions. We expect people who want to manage their diabetes to exercise and limit their intake of sugar. In the same way, we can ask chemically dependent people to change their attitudes and actions.

The Minnesota Model manages to hold contrasting ideas in a creative, fruitful balance. It asks chemically dependent people to admit their powerlessness over alcohol or other drugs. At the same time, the model calls on recovering people to reclaim their personal power: to make decisions based less on feeling and more on reflection, to learn that they are not victims, and to choose behaviors and attitudes that promote recovery. Calling alcoholism a disease still sounds a call for self-care and personal responsibility for one's actions.

At the Same Time, Chemical Dependency Transcends
The Disease Concept

We need not let the disease concept limit our understanding. Chemical dependency is both a behavior disorder and a disease. Vaillant notes that "in our attempts to *understand* and to *study* alcoholism, it behooves us to employ the models of the social scientist and of the learning theorist. But in order to *treat* alcoholics effectively, we need to invoke the model of the medical practitioner."[9]

Often the underlying question is not, *Is chemical dependency a disease?* but, *Is chemical dependency a disease that's treatable?* In many respects, we are asking not about the disease concept but about the current state of chemical dependency treatment. From this concern come related questions: Can treatment really create change and improvement? Do we have any evidence for treatment effectiveness?

Chemical dependency professionals are not alone in seeking answers to these questions. The field of mental health care faces similar dilemmas. People in both fields lack the structured protocols used in treating "real" diseases such as cancer or coronary heart disease.

The complexity of chemical dependency also makes it hard to demonstrate clear outcomes for treatment. Those outcomes must take into account subjective but intensely real indicators—variables such as quality of life, quality of personal relationships, and involvement in self-help groups. It's no wonder the treatment field looks "fuzzy" to anyone steeped in the traditional medical model.

UNDERSTANDING TREATMENT EVALUATION

Even though research on treatment outcomes is difficult, professionals who practice the Minnesota Model welcome the idea of evaluating treatment. Apart from the demands of cost containment and accountability, continuous evaluation is a necessity for treatment programs. Any program needs to answer the question, Do our efforts really make a difference?

Factors that Complicate Outcome Research

Patricia Owen, director of research at the Hazelden Foundation, points out several factors that impede research on the effectiveness of chemical dependency treatment:[10]

- Chemical dependency is difficult to diagnose. For example, clinicians may confuse alcohol abusers with those who are truly dependent on alcohol.

- Treatment plans must account for individual differences. There is no such thing as a "generic" treatment program for chemical dependency. And because there are so many different approaches to working with this condition, it is difficult to correlate specific kinds of treatment with specific outcomes.

- Among people who do enter treatment, some inevitably drop out. The reasons range from medical emergencies, family crises, or denial of the need for treatment. Others relocate and make it difficult to reach them for follow-up questions.

- As part of treatment evaluation, patients are asked whether they have remained abstinent. People who have relapsed may deny that they have returned to using chemicals. Even family members may be confused about whether the recovering person is remaining abstinent.

- It can be difficult to agree on the meaning of the word *relapse*. When does a person qualify as a treatment failure? After one relapse? Two? More?

There are other factors to consider, according to Owen. Recovery from chemical dependency requires not only abstinence but an overall change in behavior and life situation. Both of these variables are difficult to define, let alone measure. Deprived of the numbing effect of alcohol and other drugs, many recovering people confront truly distressing circumstances for the first time. Often they face huge debts or bankruptcy, loss of employment, relationships that are in shambles, or impending arrests for crimes committed when they were actively using.

These people may be attending AA regularly, enjoying a regular relationship with a sponsor, and staying abstinent. Yet when asked to rate the overall quality of their recovery, they may well report that life is worse after recovery. Are these people, then, treatment failures?

Related to this is another point: A person's rating of the quality of his or her recovery may also shift from day to day. For this reason, any study of treatment outcome is no more than a snapshot of a dynamic, sometimes volatile, situation.

The traditional tool for researching treatment outcomes is the follow-up survey. This involves contacting people who have graduated from chemical dependency treatment and asking them questions like the following: Are you attending AA meetings at least once each week? Have you abstained from using alcohol or other drugs since leaving treatment? How would you rate your overall quality of life in recovery? Often researchers conduct these surveys at various intervals after treatment, such as six, eight, and twelve months.

Such follow-up surveys have several limitations:

- Survey results cannot indicate that any program is an unqualified success. Treatment "success" is defined in many ways, and no program claims to treat all its clients successfully.

- It often takes a year or more to collect and interpret survey data. During that time, treatment programs may change. They may phase out some services and offer new ones, or they can experience a turnover in staff.

- Treatment programs are often held accountable for how long their graduates stay sober. Yet the program's direct effect ends the very minute a patient exits the doors of the treatment center.

However, there are ways to compensate for some of these difficulties. For example, researchers can insist on a high response rate to questionnaires. They can screen survey questions for clarity and consistency. And they can obtain corroborating responses from people who know the former patient.

Despite the problems of demonstrating treatment outcomes, there is a body of survey research indicating that Minnesota Model treatment can be effective. Some of the relevant findings follow.

Research from the Hazelden Consortium

During 1985 and 1986, the fourteen treatment centers that make up the Hazelden Evaluation Consortium did a joint study on treatment outcomes. These centers were carefully selected to meet certain criteria. For example, the median length of patient stay was twenty-eight days, and at least 85 percent of treated patients were discharged with staff approval. People who finished these treatment programs were surveyed at six months and twelve months after being discharged from treatment. Findings from the study are as follows:[11]

- At sixth months, 64 percent of consortium patients reported remaining abstinent. Fifty-one percent were attending AA or NA meetings weekly.

- At twelve months, the sobriety rate was 54 percent for consortium patients. Thirty-nine percent of consortium patients were attending such weekly meetings.

- Patients from the consortium were also asked to rate their overall quality of life at six months and twelve months after being discharged from treatment. After six months, 82 percent rated their lives as much or somewhat improved. And at twelve months, the comparable figure was 79 percent.

Research from the Chemical Abuse Treatment Outcome Registry (CATOR)

The Chemical Abuse Treatment Outcome Registry (CATOR) resulted from an agreement between various treatment programs in the Minneapolis-St. Paul area. These programs agreed to use a standardized set of forms and procedures to collect follow-up information on their patients. The treatment goal for these programs was to achieve total abstinence from alcohol and other drugs that are not medically indicated.

One CATOR study involved two groups of patients with different demographic characteristics. Patients in both groups were surveyed at six, twelve, eighteen, and twenty-four months after treatment discharge.

Composite figures for the two-year period showed that 58 percent of one group and 56.7 percent of the other group reported total abstinence.[12]

The "Easy Does It" Study

In his book *Easy Does It: Alcoholism Treatment Outcomes, Hazelden and the Minnesota Model*, J. Clark Laundergan presents the results of an extensive follow-up study. Laundergan surveyed 1,652 alcoholics at three intervals after treatment: four, eight, and twelve months. All these people had been treated at Hazelden, which he took to be a representative sample of Minnesota Model treatment.

Laundergan's study mentions a "Higher Power" variable, which he concluded was the most powerful predictor of improved psychological functioning after treatment. He explains there is a "strong relationship" between the Higher Power variable and AA attendance, which in turn is related to abstinence and improved psychological functioning.[13]

What Laundergan found was that activities encouraged during Minnesota Model treatment—including AA attendance, prayer, and meditation—have the greatest ability to predict abstinence following treatment.

Laundergan concludes that the Minnesota Model treatment program offered by Hazelden does yield positive outcomes. He also acknowledges that not all patients complete treatment. Moreover, not all of the people who complete treatment show major improvements.[14]

Other Findings: Treatment Reduces Medical Costs

Other studies indicate that spending money on treatment can save costs by reducing utilization of other medical care.

One example is a review of claims for federal employees covered by Aetna. This study compared 1,645 families that had a family member treated for chemical dependency with 3,598 families with no claims for chemical dependency. Before treatment, costs for medical services used by families with a chemically dependent member were twice as high as medical costs for the other families. After treatment, the costs for families with a chemically dependent member dropped dramatically. Because of this drop, researchers estimated that an employer could recoup the costs of treatment in three years.[15]

Inpatient and Outpatient Treatment

As we search for ways to reduce our rising health care costs, many turn to chemical dependency treatment as an area in which expenses can be cut. This has been one of the strategies of managed care, which often views outpatient treatment as nothing more than a cheaper version of inpatient treatment.

Advocates of managed care often cite a paper by William R. Miller and Reid K. Hester, which reviewed twenty-six controlled studies that compared the results of inpatient and outpatient treatment for alcoholism. The authors concluded that these studies did not reveal a consistent, overall advantage for inpatient treatment. Nor did the findings favor longer inpatient programs over shorter inpatient programs, or more intensive treatment interventions over less intensive interventions.[16]

Yet Miller and Hester qualified their findings with this admission:

An inherent problem in this kind of review is that inpatient

> care is not a kind of treatment—it is a setting for treatment. It is plausible that an inpatient setting may offer differential advantages with certain types of treatment or with certain kinds of clients.[17]

The authors also admitted that intensive treatment can offer special benefits for alcoholics whose condition is "severely deteriorated" and whose lives are "less socially stable" than their peers in treatment.

This is why outpatient care cannot be seen only as a less costly version of inpatient care. These two forms of treatment are not *competitive* but *complementary*. Equating inpatient care with outpatient care is comparable to asking which tool is better: a Phillips screwdriver or a flathead? In isolation, the question is without meaning. Some tools are appropriate for a specific job; others are not. The same consideration applies when choosing a form of treatment.

The Costs of Not Treating Chemical Dependency

Any discussion about the costs of treatment must take into account another consideration: the costs of *not* treating chemical dependency. Liver disease, cancers, HIV, hypertension, and injuries are some of the long-term consequences of chemical dependency that goes untreated.

H. J. Harwood made this point in a thorough comparison of treatment costs to the overall economic costs of alcohol and drug abuse. In 1980, Harwood estimated that the total cost of chemical dependency in 1983 would be $177 billion. For the same year, he projected that less than $17 billion would be spent on treatment.[18]

James S. Kemper, Jr., a recovering alcoholic and founder of the Kemper Group of insurance companies, established an Employee Assistance Plan for alcoholic employees in 1962. He concluded that the "most expensive way to handle alcoholics is to fire or ignore them. The most profitable and effective way is to help them recover."[19]

Helen Corrothers, president of the American Corrections Association, adds her perspective:

> Perhaps the greatest single problem we find among individuals who enter the corrections system is substance abuse. While some of the offenses may be drug offenses, such as drug possession or drug trafficking, others, such as burglaries, are committed in order to obtain funds to acquire drugs. Also, some studies have found that nearly 80 percent of offenders were under the influence of drugs at the time of arrest and/or during the commission of their offense.[20]

Promise for the Future: The Recovery Pathways Model

To date, most outcome studies have tried to answer the question, How has this group of people changed since leaving treatment? Focusing on this question can lead us astray. A more powerful question is, Are the individuals we've treated continuing to get better? We are beginning to answer that question through the recovery pathways model.

The Minnesota Model is a rehabilitation model. It exists to promote long-term change. Chemical dependency presents us with the kinds of problems faced by other branches of rehabilitation medicine. People with chronic low-back pain, for example, may have to live with their problem for a lifetime. Treatment for this condition, then, does not focus upon ridding people of their condition but helping them reduce the acute episodes of back pain and improve their overall health.

This example raises an important question in evaluating rehabilitation care. Would we say that rehabilitation care has failed if a person with a chronic back condition experiences an isolated incident of acute pain? Probably not. The question of treatment effectiveness does not hinge on this kind of black-and-white, simplistic thinking: either back pain is "cured," or it is not. Far more essential are the individual's path of recovery over time and overall progress in learning how to live well with chronic back pain.

According to the recovery pathways model, the same perspective applies to people recovering from chemical dependency. Here the goal is continuous assessment of the individual's condition over time—periodically dipping into the stream of events in that person's life. We cannot reach that goal from an oversimplified orientation: Did she stay abstinent or not? Did he attend an AA meeting every week or not?

We need new assessments that plot the individual's experience of sobriety on a continuum, perhaps on a scale from 1 to 100. Such an assessment considers not only the recovering person but his or her surrounding support systems: relationships with family members, friends, co-workers, employers, and social services in the community.

This calls for certain practical strategies. First, we need a way to stay in periodic contact with graduates of treatment programs. One possibility is phone contact and occasional one-to-one interviews conducted by a case manager. We also need a concrete understanding of the individual's readiness for various types of treatment—anything from inpatient care to aftercare services. Included here is careful attention to the severity of a person's problem with chemical use.

Finally, the recovery pathways model calls for flexible routes through the whole array of treatment services, not a linear progression from detoxification to inpatient care to aftercare. The people who provide such varying services need to be in constant contact with one another, coordinating the overall treatment plan for the recovering person. Here the goals of treatment and program evaluation merge beautifully. Follow-up interviews with clients can serve as both assessment and aftercare.

In some ways, the recovery pathways model contrasts with current practices of Minnesota Model programs. Yet in its insistence on "progress, not perfection" and "caring, not curing" it takes us back to the core perspectives of the Minnesota Model. And though this option is still in its early stages, it holds great promise for the future of chemical dependency treatment.

CHAPTER SEVEN

Challenges and Possible Futures

There's a saying attributed to Marshall Field, founder of the retail store chain that bears his name: "Bringing about change in an organization is like walking through a wall of human flesh backwards, dragging a goat in a canoe."[1] Yet promoting organizational change is one of the many challenges now confronting practitioners of the Minnesota Model.

The purpose of this chapter is to speculate about how the Minnesota Model may change as it continues into the next century. And we can underline the word *speculate*, since this task has many inherent difficulties. Perhaps no one summed it up better than Yogi Berra: "Prediction is difficult, especially when it's about the future."

PUSHING PUBLIC POLICY BEYOND THE WAR ON DRUGS

One of the most immediate challenges for advocates of the Minnesota Model is to challenge the thinking currently represented by the "war on drugs."

Governments make a common mistake by trying to curb the supply of illicit, mind-altering chemicals. These efforts are fundamentally flawed. Even when interdiction efforts do succeed in reducing the supply of a drug, many addicts will switch to another chemical. Moreover, users of illicit drugs make up only a fraction of our population. In terms of their human costs, alcohol and nicotine are far more costly to our society. And yet the war on drugs allocates no funds to fight these addictions.

The war on drugs can also stigmatize the people who do become addicted to illegal chemicals. Stereotypes about these people are too easily reinforced: namely, that they are mainly lower-income latino or black crack addicts, and so on. These stereotypes allow us to reject drug users as the enemy without ever becoming involved in efforts to treat them.

The war on drugs too easily becomes a war on *people* who use drugs.

This failed war has resulted in an adversarial relationship between government officials and treatment providers. Our best hope for the next century is to abandon this approach in favor of a dialogue that serves the long-term interests of all parties.

RESPONDING TO MANAGED CARE

The tenuous relationship between treatment providers and managed care was examined in chapter 4. Here, too, the future of the Minnesota Model hinges on establishing more cooperative relationships. Treatment centers cannot afford to ignore the realities of cost containment. Nor can managed care succeed if it ignores the features and benefits of rehabilitative care.

One solution is for both parties to budge a little. Treatment centers can do a better job of providing data about diagnoses and outcomes. They can also expand use of outpatient care when that is appropriate. And managed care companies can learn more about the nature of chemical dependency. In the process, they could make more informed decisions about which kinds of treatment will be most effective for a given individual.

CREATING NEW OPTIONS FOR FINANCING CARE

The challenge of helping people find ways to pay for treatment will continue into the foreseeable future. When it comes to inpatient care, we may be on the verge of a two-tiered system: one for people who can afford to pay for their own treatment, and one for people who can't. Involvement by the federal government—including some form of national health care—could alter this equation. It could be the only way to bring chemical dependency treatment to the thirty million Americans who are uninsured or underinsured.

De facto rationing of health care along financial lines may also ration care along demographic lines as well. The people who will be excluded from treatment are more likely to be members of racial and ethnic minorities, female, and young.

Faced with these trends, entrepreneurs who will find a way to provide treatment outside of the traditional health care system could emerge. If the United States does adopt some form of national health care, it's possible that chemical dependency treatment may not be covered. In that case, treatment providers may contract directly with employers, offering to provide chemical dependency services to employees and their families for a fixed fee. Essentially, these providers would operate the way HMOs and PPOs do today.

This arrangement would put treatment programs much more in control of their own destiny—while increasing their financial risks. At present, we have no clear picture of the amount of those risks; moreover, treatment centers like Hazelden have traditionally been concerned about mixing clinical judgment with financial risk.

Another option is already being tried by some large employers. These companies are removing the dollars spent for chemical dependency from their insurance budgets and reallocating them to their employee assistance programs. This is the way treatment was often funded before there was any insurance coverage for chemical dependency services: the employee assistance programs basically wrote out the checks for treatment.

Helping Patients with Mounting Problems

The nature of the problems presented by people who enter treatment has shifted radically over the past decade. Today, for example, more of those people are poor, homeless, and victims of racism—a trend that will no doubt continue as these social problems worsen.

Highly addictive drugs, including crack cocaine and "ice," an amphetamine, have also had their impact. Even the "mellow" marijuana of the 1960s is gone. During the late 1960s the THC content of marijuana was typically about 1 to 2 percent. Today's crop may contain up to 12 percent THC. (THC is the mood-altering agent present in marijuana.)

The relatively low price of crack and ice makes these chemicals attractive to adolescents, who may become dealers themselves. This phenomenon creates yet another challenge to the rehabilitation model. Drug use can arrest the cognitive, emotional, and social development of young people. They simply may never develop a history of stable family relationships and employment. When that happens, the job of the treatment center becomes helping young people develop crucial life skills—"habilitation" instead of "rehabilitation."

Comorbidity problems, or *dual disorders*, represent another growing issue for treatment centers. These terms refer to people who not only are addicted to chemicals but have some other condition that demands treatment. Examples of the latter are mental illness and AIDS. It is essential for treatment programs to come to terms with this increasingly visible issue, since negative outcomes for alcoholics and drug addicts are often related to comorbidity problems.

The presence of more troubled patients must lead us to become more skilled at screening for chemical dependency. For instance, anyone who seeks help from a social service agency could be screened for alcohol or drug abuse. Making this work presupposes that we have effective screening methods, which is often not the case.

Finally, we can match the patient with the program. Currently we often assign people to outpatient treatment who should be in intensive residential programs; or, conversely, we use residential care because a viable outpatient program is inaccessible. And some people are entering inpatient programs who need a more thorough detoxification or hospitalization for another illness. This is a little like scheduling a person who needs open-heart surgery for a routine physical. Our efforts at program-patient management are unsystematic and prescientific. The challenge we face is to develop an appropriate level for each individual.

PROMOTING SELF-CARE AND MUTUAL HELP

A significant portion of the $700 billion spent each year in the United States on health care goes for the treatment of conditions that are greatly affected by lifestyle choice. For example, diet, exercise, use of seat belts, and stress management are key factors in a host of chronic illnesses ranging from heart disease to cancer. Also included here is addiction to nicotine, alcohol, and other drugs.

Many of our health care costs, then, result from behaviors that can be modified. And the key to changing such behaviors is medical treatment that promotes self-care. Here the Minnesota Model has a distinct advantage, since it has been promoting self-care as an element of treatment since the early 1950s. Along with AA, the Minnesota Model discovered the importance of mutual help groups in promoting behavior change. This movement reflects the increasing acceptance of personal responsibility for our own physical and mental health.

Yet we by no means have pat answers. Persuading people to buckle their seat belts regularly is hard enough. Helping them manage a long-term chronic illness presents a challenge of far greater complexity.

"REVISIONING" THE MINNESOTA MODEL

With the success of the Minnesota Model have come problems that show few signs of going away soon. As Anderson has pointed out, many of these concern our very conception of the model:[2]

- The Minnesota Model works for many people. Yet we cannot

explain how many people it truly helps or how well it works for them. Consequently, discussions of the Minnesota Model are often divided into two camps: vocal supporters and equally vocal detractors.

- Chemical dependency treatment draws on two epistemologies—that is, two ways of knowing about the world. One is the scientific perspective introduced to the model by physicians and clinical psychologists. Another is the experiential, commonsense wisdom exemplified by AA. Such a heady mixture of perspectives can be a strength if we use them to complement each other. Yet this combination can also be explosive and polarizing.

- Our understanding of treatment in general, and the Minnesota Model in particular, is prescientific. There is an urgent need for research. Yet those who try to conduct controlled research in this area are dogged by methodological problems. Treatment methods are highly variable, ranging from individual counseling and group therapy to informal interaction with peers. Treatment also takes place in multiple settings, ranging from intensive residential care to outpatient services, halfway houses, and aftercare programs. It is difficult to sort out and quantify the effects of all these interventions. The concept of "recovery," too, is difficult to define, going well beyond mere abstinence. And denying some people treatment in order to assign them to control groups for research purposes poses huge ethical problems.

- Some critics of the Minnesota Model are uneasy about treatment centers that hire recovering alcoholics and drug addicts as counselors. Such counselors are often powerful role models for people in early recovery and can empathize with patients in a way that is difficult for nonrecovering people to do. Some outsiders, however, see recovering counselors as lacking the qualifications to provide medical and psychological treatment, a sign that the treatment field as a whole has yet to be fully professionalized.

- Programs based on the Minnesota Model traditionally offer treatment lasting around four weeks. Many practitioners of the model argue that this length of stay is necessary to achieve a level of intensity that promotes long-term behavior change. Yet there are overwhelming pressures from health insurers and managed care organizations to shorten treatment stays. Again, there are questions to answer: Can a Minnesota Model program be offered in fewer than twenty-eight or thirty days? Is seven, fourteen, or twenty-one days enough?

- The Minnesota Model is free for the taking. No one regulates the use of the name "Minnesota Model," and programs with widely varying philosophies and levels of quality have appropriated it. The question is, What distinguishes the Minnesota Model from other forms of treatment? When can a treatment center legitimately call itself a Minnesota Model program? And at what level of modification does it become something other than the Minnesota Model? Even professionals who can agree on a general definition of the Minnesota Model can disagree about which programs are true Minnesota Models in practice.

In reality, very few people understand the Minnesota Model. In a way, *Minnesota Model* has become a generic term, like "Kleenex." People might use it to describe what they do in treatment, even though their activities have no relationship to anything resembling a Minnesota Model. For example, programs with one counselor and a member of the clergy can call themselves "multidisciplinary."

Visitors at long-standing Minnesota Model programs such as Hazelden often describe the atmosphere as "magical." They sense, in a direct and intuitive way, that the total environment is therapeutic in a way that goes beyond their understanding. Yet what's often at work behind this environment is a specific set of procedures, standards, expectations, and goals. Even more fundamental are the core perspectives behind the program—especially the idea that chemically dependent people deserve to be treated with dignity. None of it happens by magic.

One of the strengths of the Minnesota Model, its flexibility and openness to change, has also become a weakness. Today we see evidence of the very human tendency to take a powerful tool and apply it to almost any aspect of the human condition.

ADAPTING THE MINNESOTA MODEL TO OTHER COUNTRIES AND CULTURES

Visitors from other cultures who come to a Minnesota Model treatment program are sometimes shocked by what they see. One person from an African country who visited Hazelden wanted to know how many alcoholics we executed! The incident is extreme, but it points out how unusual the concept of respect and dignity for chemically dependent people really is.

Western countries still struggle to accept this idea too. Great Britain, for example, has a large number of Alcoholics Anonymous groups and treatment centers based on the Minnesota Model. Yet alcoholics and addicts there are still widely stigmatized.

The United States is an exception in another respect: most other developed countries offer some form of national health care. Anyone who wants to establish a Minnesota Model program in these countries faces the immediate problem of how to fit it into that national system. In the United States, the solution has been straightforward; with some significant exceptions, Minnesota Model treatment programs have developed outside the aegis of the federal government. In many other nations, this would not be an option, since the government drives the health care system. And, as we know from history, governmental policies relating to chemical dependency can be quixotic.

Even so, the Minnesota Model has an important constituency overseas. England, Ireland, Sweden, Canada, Brazil, and Iceland—

all have treatment centers based on the model. Often these centers are the brainchildren of individual entrepreneurs operating outside the national health care system.

A related issue surfaces when we talk about applying the model across cultures. Core aspects of the Minnesota Model—respect, dignity, and the rehabilitation perspective—are appropriate for all people. The model represents a unified theory about chemical dependency. And one dynamic of this theory is that certain aspects of the condition apply universally, across differences in class, race, or religion.

At the same time, the Minnesota Model has yet to demonstrate its cultural universality. The old stereotype of AA members as white, middle-aged males still has much basis in fact. And the majority of clients at Minnesota Model treatment centers such as Hazelden are middle-class and white.

This has prompted programs to become more aware of individual differences. Such efforts are not entirely new to the Minnesota Model, since it has emphasized individualized treatment planning from its inception. The aim, however, is to go well beyond such crude generalities as "Women need special help with assertiveness" or "Native Americans are already in tune with the idea of spirituality."

RESPONDING TO CONTINUING IGNORANCE AND STIGMA

The whole issue of stigma and shame has never left chemically dependent people. Today they still face ostracism, moral condemnation, punishment, and job discrimination. In the waning years of the twentieth century we continue to face a regression to the way of thinking that stigmatizes alcoholics and other addicts. The very language used to discuss this issue—such as the "war" on drugs—betrays a moralistic, punitive stance.

In the United States, attitudes about drinking and drug use are ambivalent and confused. There is little or no agreement on what constitutes responsible use of alcohol and other drugs. At the same time, Americans use drugs, both licit and illicit, in huge numbers.

113

The stereotype of alcoholics and drug addicts as weak-willed moral failures continues to hamper our efforts to provide treatment and shape public policy.

The past forty years of American history presents us with a contradiction. On the one hand, thousands of people with chemical dependency have found a path toward sobriety in the Minnesota Model. Popular interest in the Twelve Steps has skyrocketed, as evidenced by the number of self-help groups and best-selling books on recovery. At the same time, the United States is building more jails and populating them with people who are chemically dependent. As in the case of Prohibition, there is almost no relationship between national policy and the behavior of the population.

Part of the reason is that most of the people who use alcohol and other drugs—about 90 percent of them—never become chemically dependent. And in other countries across the world the condition is still stigmatized and ignored, much as it was in the United States fifty years ago. The continuing challenge is for treatment providers to educate and inform each generation. "In a very real sense," notes Anderson, "alcoholism does not exist until the community says it does, and comprehensive treatment programs will not be fully available until public support is fully mobilized."[3]

Return to Innovation And The Grass-Roots Spirit

Anyone who studies the history of the earliest Minnesota Model programs can get a sense of how heady and exciting the programs were when they began. In those days there was no licensing and little regulation of treatment programs. Treatment providers didn't worry about insurance coverage or managed care. Those who created the model walked in uncharted territory.

Nelson Bradley's recollection of the atmosphere at Willmar State Hospital is an example: "The enthusiasm we had at Willmar was really something—besides the energy—everyone was caught up in this—we ate and slept it. We talked about it in the coffee shop—we never let go of it."[4]

This kind of environment attracts certain kinds of people—free spirits, gadflies, entrepreneurs—whatever we want to call them. And today's chemical dependency environment, replete with formal bureaucracies, often attracts different kinds of people. Unlike the Minnesota Model, AA has largely resisted this fate.

Perhaps Minnesota Model advocates have grown lazy. We rested on our laurels as thousands of treatment programs adopted the model. We lost the excitement of launching a new social movement.

The future of the Minnesota Model—and of treatment in general—depends to a great extent on whether we can return to the spirit of grass-roots advocacy. What we've discovered is that the perspectives of the Minnesota Model have yet to be forged into lasting public policy.

What it takes is a rare combination of grass-roots organizing, professional support, and a larger culture that is ready for the message. Recent history tells us that popular social movements grow from the ground up, long before they gain governmental acceptance. Slowly, these movements gain momentum through support from business and professional leaders. At the risk of oversimplifying, we can say that self-help comes first, and public policy follows. A telling example is Sen. Harold Hughes, who, as mentioned earlier, publicly admitted his own alcoholism and then conducted open hearings on the topic across the country. His efforts led to federal legislation often referred to as the Hughes Act and the establishment of the NIAAA.

Charges that Twelve Step groups promote political passivity are contradicted by our present efforts to shape public policy. Yet the tradition of anonymity that the Minnesota Model inherited from AA—a core principle of treatment—makes it harder to do so. Treatment professionals cannot ask recovering celebrities to go public with their stories and personally launch national fund-raising campaigns. Fortunately, some national figures like Harold Hughes and Betty Ford *have* stepped forward on their own and generated immense interest in treatment.

One more note: professionals in chemical dependency do not have a long track record of working together well. The need for us to infuse the Minnesota Model with some political muscle could perform a positive function by forcing us to change that.

Summing Up

Two broad visions of the Minnesota Model's future might be called a "best-case scenario" and a "worst-case scenario." The former includes ongoing success in shaping public policy; new gains in providing high-quality, cost-effective treatment; and comprehensive public education about the nature of treatment and chemical dependency. If this scenario becomes reality, it will reaffirm the model's earliest premise: that chemical dependency is treatable, chemically dependent people deserve to be treated with dignity, and treatment is a sound financial investment.

The worst-case scenario is that Minnesota Model programs will be seen as a temporary aberration in the treatment of alcoholics and addicts. Chemical dependency services will be available only to people who can afford to pay for them out-of-pocket, and there will be only a handful of treatment centers left in the country. People with chemical dependency will again be consigned to jails, prisons, or mental wards. We will return to the social environment that greeted the creators of the Minnesota Model in the 1950s.

Fortunately, the Minnesota Model is flexible enough to accommodate many of the changes that need to be made to ensure its survival into the twenty-first century. Adherents of the model can "bend" its particulars—such as length of stay or treatment activities—while leaving its core perspectives intact.

Remaining in the forefront are the personal examples of men, women, and young people who want to overcome their addictions. Our ultimate allegiance is to them—not to a set of theoretical assumptions or policies and procedures. Whether some discrete entity known as the Minnesota Model survives into the twenty-first century is less important than whether chemically dependent people are able to walk what Bill W. called the "Broad Highway"—the path to lifelong sobriety.

As we reflect on the fate of the Minnesota Model, it is time for us to learn again, and to remember. Recovery from addiction is about people—our brothers and sisters, mothers and fathers, friends and co-workers—regaining sanity one person at a time, one day at a time.

Reflections on the Minnesota Model— An Interview with Daniel J. Anderson

Daniel J. Anderson, Ph.D., is president emeritus of the Hazelden Foundation. He joined Hazelden as its director in 1961 and served in that position for twenty-five years. Before coming to Hazelden, Anderson worked closely with Nelson Bradley at Willmar State Hospital, one of three "laboratories" that developed the Minnesota Model of chemical dependency treatment.

In this interview, Anderson speaks about a wide range of topics related to treatment and the nature of chemical dependency. The interviewer's comments and questions appear in italics.*

Say a little about the nature of addiction.

Nobody knows the locus of addiction. Is it in the person? It is psychological? Is it physiological, constitutional? Is it in the culture? Actually, it's all over. And even if researchers find more and more evidence for a biological, physiological cause, that doesn't work all by itself. You have to have other environmental factors. And we wind up developing complex biopsychosocial models to explain something that we don't understand very well.

The Minnesota Model never focused primarily on a deep knowledge of etiology. We just made certain assumptions and tried to help

---

*Interview with Daniel J. Anderson by Scott Edelstein.

people modify their behavior. To hell with finding the underlying cause of addiction. There may or may not be anything there. Our goal was to try to help modify or arrest behavior, and to do what worked. "Where it doesn't itch, don't scratch" was the initial philosophy. Forget all of that deep theoretical stuff.

But that's changed.

It's changed, for example, in dealing with comorbidity. And notice that it's called "dual disability," or "comorbidity." You can have a mental illness associated with your addiction, and there doesn't necessarily have to be a causal relationship. But one condition can sure interfere with the other condition, with its treatment and maintenance. So you try to treat both of these conditions.

That's not new. We were doing that in the decade of the 1950s at Willmar State Hospital. We were happy to see alcoholics who had other mental illness problems, because we thought we understood those problems. It was the addiction we didn't understand. What we gave up was thinking that the addiction is symptomatic of something else: treat the something else and the symptoms will go away. I don't even deny alcoholism may well be symptomatic, initially. But it takes on an autonomy over time. Criminal behavior in a causal sense may result from weak ego, the fact that your mother didn't love you, or any number of things. But once you've become real good at it, that becomes an autonomous kind of behavior in its own right. Even if you could modify other thinking, other emotions, you're still stuck with learning to modify your well-learned criminal behavior.

And even if you could address the initial causes, you would still have the current behavior.

Right, but see, it's all complex. And the trouble with the Minnesota Model is that it, too, is far more complex than it looks. There's this terrible problem of reductionism, and people who try to be scientific or state theoretical problems often do a bunch of reductionist things.

The Minnesota Model may work to some degree, but for reasons we don't even understand. We're just making assumptions. Today, I think the roughest problem in addiction is that we are into biological psychiatry. We're trying to explain obsessive-compulsive behavior through brain scans. We are trying to explain the genetic histories of alcoholics, which makes it look like there are a bunch of little cells in the brain fooling around there producing all this behavior. And I think we are going to find all kinds of people with those same cellular modifications, and some will have alcoholism and some won't.

So we have to think about addiction being multiply determined. But once you've got it, it becomes a primary illness in its own right. Now, if there's another problem like psychosis interfering with treatment, I think you can work on the psychosis first and do something to clear that up. But on the other hand, you can deal with any number of emotional or mental health problems once you have your addiction under control. It helps a lot to sober up first, and have some way of remaining sober.

You've begun with a number of existential questions, and it seems that the basis of Alcoholics Anonymous and any treatment program based on it is grappling with some of these existential questions. It also seems that a number of critics of the Minnesota Model and AA miss this whole point. I'd like you to talk about that if you could.

AA uses certain language: *alcoholism is a disease of body, mind, and spirit.* And only a spiritual experience can change that. They're talking not about curing the disease, but arresting it. And to do that you have to develop another mind-set and ask some questions: What am I living for? What am I doing here? What are my real values? Do I really want to keep living this way?

I don't think we fully understand all this. The minute you start talking about spiritual stuff, people get all mixed up and think it's religion. It's not. As a spiritual philosophy, that basic philosophy of AA can cross cultures and religious values. And it works for people who can understand it. AA expresses it so terribly simply: You have a problem that you've been explaining to yourself in all kinds of ways. But really you have an addiction, and you have to accept that.

These are some things that you can do, if you'll take a chance, and that gets into values. This is what we learned from AA. Everybody thinks that Higher Power means a well-developed theological concept of a God. For an alcoholic just sobering up, all it means is this: Something is stronger than I am—booze is one good example—and I need help to cope with it.

To actually realize you have human limitations and to be willing to live with that fact—this is one tremendous existential secret: My God, I'm human; I have to join the human race and be a limited person. But see, what our common culture teaches is the opposite: "Out of the night that covers me, dark as the pit from pole to pole, I thank whatever gods may be, for my unconquerable soul." I will, I can, overcome everything, as William Ernest Henley put so well in his poem *Invictus*.

If only everyone wanted to enough, everyone would be president of the United States.

Right. But if you look around, you see that very few people get out of this world alive. Human limitation comes built in. That's what the recovering alcoholic learns.

There's a paradox here, one that's expressed in an AA story about the alcoholic who says, "I'm an egomaniac with an inferiority complex." I think that's just beautiful. Because addicts can demonstrate massive inadequacy and massive grandiosity all at the same time. The drunken skid row bum trying to direct traffic in Manhattan is the best example. The cops are going to pick him up, but he's helping keep the city going! AA has an awareness that I don't think can be captured in testing, or in looking at brain interactions and stuff like that.

Today the Minnesota Model is coming under attack from a number of different sides. Alternatives to AA are cropping up, such as Rational Recovery and Women for Sobriety. Meanwhile insurance companies are saying, Who needs four weeks of inpatient treatment? What does all this bode for the future?

That's a complex question, and I can give only a partial response. First of all, the Minnesota Model, this comprehensive model, worked better than anything else we had. So it started to grow. Today there are over 7,000 treatment programs in the United States, and we started with a handful. With that kind of growth, you need a multidisciplinary group of people to do treatment. What it's all supposed to do initially is accept people with chemical dependency as people with an illness and bring them into the health care system.

With any kind of growth of a new health care system, though, people finally get together to agree on what they are doing. And then you start licensing people and accrediting programs. We had that throughout the decade of the 1970s, especially once the government got involved trying to do something about treatment. But that brought in all kinds of entrepreneurs: profit-making outfits, hospitals that had empty beds. Then they finally discover alcoholics: once you learn how to "detox" them, they're not bad. Gall bladders can be more troublesome. Not only that, you can charge these people a lot of money and you can pay off the mortgage on the hospital—a lot of hospitals. And so the costs kept going up. The accreditation and licensing costs and the cost of inpatient hospital treatment went up. At the same time there weren't too many scientific studies. You know—real science with control group and random assignments, something that's quite hard for a small program to do.

123

Then the 1960s ushered in all kinds of things, including the drug culture and a basic attitude of "I have a right to do my own thing. I have a right to alter my internal psychological environment any damn time I want to." And that attitude has stayed with us.

What happens as this passes on from generation to generation is that we wind up with a big focus on the illegal drugs that are coming into the country. So we watch television and see the police officers with bulldozers knocking down a crack house. We see "crack mothers" and "crack babies." We hear about the tremendous money and corruption of the illegal drug trade. So we get worried and launch a terrible war on drugs, and we get mad at all those people who take them: "Shoot 'em all, let God decide what to do with them. Treatment doesn't work for everybody anyway, so throw them in the slammer. That works."

That's where I started in 1950! The same attitudes are returning: "Addiction is really not a disease anyway. If you punish them enough, they'll catch on. Look at so-and-so who quit drinking, so why can't you?"

Aren't you suggesting that people basically don't want to deal with this problem?

Right. It's too complicated. It doesn't fit into my simple mind-set.

The best thing about this Minnesota Model is that it's a good model for all chronic illnesses. But what we don't want to cope with, what we're not taught to cope with, is chronic illness. We have this quick-fix mentality—the acute-intervention, fee-for-service, be-cured-or-die model. That's what people want.

Like taking a TV in to get it fixed.

Right. We can't stand chronicity. This to me is the greatest denial of all. In the developed nations of the world, 80 percent of the people who are sick with anything are sick with a chronic illness. And what do people with chronic illnesses do? They do the same crazy thing that alcoholics do: they deny the problem.

Few people really like drunks or drug addicts anyway. But there are different ways of interpreting that pathological behavior. And see, that's what we do in the Minnesota Model. We see a bunch of crazy behavior, but the interpretation, the spin we put on it, is that the crazy behavior is part of an addiction. If we can deal with the addiction, we can modify a lot of that behavior. For the vast majority of addicted people, when they sober up and find a way to stay sober, they change their values and become human beings again. They start using the ethical codes that they should.

And this is the great tragedy. All of these factors come together in the 1980s. And I call it Social Darwinism, survival of the fittest, get rid of the unfit: We don't like crazy people. We don't like alcoholics. We don't like chronic illness, either.

By the way, I think the polar opposite of Social Darwinism is an expanded humanitarianism. That's the other problem today. Back in the 1940s Marty Mann went around the country saying, look, alcoholism is a disease. We know what the symptoms are now. Alcoholics are sick people, they want help, and they're worth helping, no matter what they look like. And there were examples of skid row bums who were once lawyers and judges and doctors. She was saying this to a society that was still in the Social Darwinism mind-set with very limited humanitarian concerns.

But notice today, even with an increased sense of humanitarianism, if you decide to be charitable about something, you've got the chronic physical and mental illnesses, the homeless, the uninsured, AIDS, various racial minority groups, etc., etc. You see it all when you go through your mail, when you watch the starving kids on television. Pretty soon, you ask what's for dinner and you block it all out. It's just terrible. So today addiction has to compete with all kinds of worthy causes.

Reflections on the Minnesota Model

That brings us to public education. The Minnesota Model is not something you explain just once. You have to keep explaining it over and over again.

At first we thought, we've been running around talking about this for ten years now and that's enough. People must have caught on now. They didn't, and we never communicated the model to newer generations very well.

So what's the task for the future, in terms of education?

We have to do it all over again. I think we need to tell people how much money they're losing. We're throwing addicts in prison. We're building more prisons all the time and filling them up. But it can cost $27,000 a year to put somebody in the slammer. For that you could send them to Harvard or Yale! Or you could send them to treatment. In fact, you could develop treatment programs that would be cheaper than that.

By the way, the criminal justice system fails to assess people properly to see if they have a chemical dependency problem. And yet we know 50 to 80 percent of the people in prison do.

Back to education again: What do we need to do to prepare for the future?

One thing is to keep working on the biological basis of addiction. The idea is to understand it better. There are different types of addiction; it's not a unitary phenomenon. And by understanding those typologies, we can make progress. In most sciences that's finally what you do. For example, there's late-onset diabetes and early-onset diabetes: child diabetes differs from adult diabetes. Schizophrenia can be divided into three or four types. So far alcoholism has never been understood that way. All of the talk about the alpha, beta, delta, gamma, and epsilon types of alcoholism—it never did work. Differences that don't make any difference aren't differences.

There's still the hope of developing a nonaddictive drug that will reduce craving—and maybe some of the pain of living. Remember, this has been the great hope of mankind: to find something that we can ingest or take in that will reduce pain, increase energy, produce sleep, and give us whatever feelings we want to have.

The other thing involves improving education and developing public policies. We're only now beginning to admit that alcohol and nicotine are the most devastating drugs in terms of morbidity and mortality. That's a new idea. These are socially acceptable drugs that have been around forever, and nobody wants to face up to the problems they introduce. Once a culture has learned about alcohol and how to make it, there's no getting rid of it. No matter how illegal you make it, you can still make it in your basement with dandelions. We're never going to stamp out dandelions.

The cultural sanctions that regulate drinking have also been lost. People are losing their cultural roots, all over. Prevention, doing something about all of this, is going to depend upon the whole culture developing a sense of responsibility. That's the best thing about those television clips of the police with the Caterpillar tractor mowing down the crack houses. There's a woman there, shaking her finger at the cop and saying, "You people should have been here five years ago and done something about this."

We've become self-centered, egocentric, doing our own thing. We've lost our sense of community. To me, a terrible question about the future, and the one we can't answer yet, is this: Do we have enough humanitarianism to be personally responsible for ourselves as members of a community?

My greatest fear, by the way, relates to what I call technology transfer and exchange. If you're really going to educate people about prevention and treatment, you have to have something to tell them. It has to have some scientific basis. You've got to do the research. Then you've got to package it to go out into communities. Then you have to tell all of the significant stakeholders in the community—not just the schools, but parents, the medical system, the criminal justice system, the recreational system—all of these people. And they have to have a sense of personal responsibility, a sense of what to say, what to do, and how to communicate. But mainly what they need is a sense of what to do when they see trouble: Who can I refer to? Who'll help me? Then the whole system of developing something to help the community has to be tested, in some scientific fashion, to see whether it works.

The trouble is that when it comes to chemical dependency treatment, we are dealing with soft science, not hard science. So you wind up asking, What's the best prevention education? As you know, that's a can of worms; we don't have complete answers yet. But we have to live with that. Technology transfer and exchange go very slowly.

You mentioned your experience in developing the treatment program at Willmar State Hospital in the early 1950s. Could you talk a little bit more about this?

My answer to that needs to go back a ways. Social Darwinism didn't begin to change until after World War II—about 1947. I was working my way through St. Thomas College as an attendant at Hastings State Hospital in Hastings, Minnesota. I stayed there because I could get a hundred and twenty bucks a month along with room and board and I could work the night shift so I could go to school days or afternoons. In the middle of this, in 1947 or 1948, Nelson Bradley, a Canadian physician, started on his way to surgery residency at Ann Arbor, Michigan. His car broke down in Minneapolis. Eventually he met Ralph Rossen, the superintendent of Hastings State Hospital, and Ralph talked him into going to work at Hastings. He didn't even have an opening for a physician. As I understand it, Bradley worked as an RN at first.

Anyway, I was working my way through college, and a church in St. Paul was sending some of their college students to work for the summer, like I did, at Hastings State Hospital. This led to an exposé of the snake pits. Remember, all state hospitals in the state [at that time] were snake pits. Ralph Rossen said, look, we've got to clean up these places. By the way, there's no money. There's no staff, no programs. There's nothing.

But from Ralph Rossen we [also] got something different. He said, you've got to think about one mental patient. Don't think about all nine hundred here. We've got to think about what we can do today for one patient. We're talking about taking camisoles and restraints off of them. We're talking about getting them all dressed, a hundred patients on a unit, and taking them out for a walk once a day.

This was exhausting. The had to get their shoes on, and they had to get dresses on the women. This was the beginning of cleaning up the snake pits.

Well, clinical psychology was just beginning back then. I graduated from St. Thomas and I didn't know what to do, and it looked like I had to have a master's degree. Meanwhile, Bradley, in 1950, got a chance to be superintendent at Willmar—another snake pit. He wanted me to go up with him and try to do something about that; we both caught that fervor from Ralph Rossen. So I went up there with him in the summer of 1950. And we started doing the stuff: opening up doors for mental patients, improving the food, taking off the camisoles and cuffs, making life more bearable for them.

And we weren't even thinking about alcoholism. On the way to Willmar in 1950, Bradley said to me, geez, Dan, they've got inebs up there and I don't know anything about them. I was Bradley's gofer, his scut man, so I said, don't worry, I'll read the literature, grandiosity coming out of each pore of my body. Well, I read the literature and I went into a depression. Just terrible. Karl Menninger from the Menninger clinic said words to this effect in 1948: If I had a young relative destined to become mentally ill, I'd sooner have him become schizophrenic than alcoholic, because there's some hope for schizophrenia. And we knew there was no hope for schizophrenics at the time; they went out in a coffin when they left the state hospital, though once in a while you'd get a spontaneous recovery.

So we started working on better treatment. We were discharging young schizophrenics. We had a program for them, a good farmer running the state hospital farm. He took these young guys under his wing and they started getting well; gave them some medications, a little something, and they were recovering. We were discharging old mental patients to nursing homes—we were doing all of this stuff. Meanwhile, we had these inebs—mainly men, a few women—locked up on the admitting psych unit.

Then some AA people come out to talk to us, recovering alcoholics from the Twin Cities. We kept talking about alcoholism and AA, and I was reading the literature. By 1952, I was telling Bradley, look, there's been a bunch of physicians trying to help alcoholics get well physically, and it's not working too well. There's a bunch of clergy people who've been trying to sober them up, save them, and give them ethics; that isn't working too well, either. Then we have a bunch of social workers trying to pick up alcoholics' home lives and blaming the condition on the wives, and there's a bunch of psychiatrists trying to shrink their heads. Nothing's working. So I said, maybe we should do it all: we'd put it all together, maybe we'd fix them up physically and try to help them with social problems. If they were mentally ill, we would shrink their heads a little bit. And we would also include AA and members of the clergy. In short, we decided that we had to have an interdisciplinary staff and create a total learning environment for alcoholics. We also agreed that alcoholism was an illness—at least we were going to make believe it was until somebody explained it better.

But the point was this: treat alcoholics with dignity and respect. Stop blaming. We didn't know what alcoholism was, anyway, so stop blaming them. So we interviewed alcoholics over and over again. Back then we were psychoanalytically oriented, you know; we would diagnose you twenty different ways and we would find all kinds of subconscious dynamics. But finally we came to this conclusion: alcoholics come in different sizes and shapes, but what they all have in common is their addiction, and that pattern of pathological drinking just goes on and on. No matter how they explained away their drinking, there they were, plop, plop, plop—all doing the same damned thing. So we decide that what we should work on was the phenomenon of addiction. AA was right about that: what's wrong with alcoholics is that they are alcoholic.

So we started doing all this, and the patients liked it. See, the thing that's so hard to explain was this dynamic relationship with the patients. These people were skid row bums, prostitutes, and yet, Bradley said, what's wrong with these alcoholics is that they're ignorant. They think they know alcohol and what it does to them. In those days alcohol was supposed to be a stimulant; they didn't know it was a depressant.

So we started giving lectures. We were about one page ahead of the patients, and there we were giving lectures. Here's the physiology of alcoholism, here are some of the psychological things we know about it.

At the same time, we were learning things from AA. At first we were thinking about alcoholism in terms of major pathology, as paranoia and schizophrenia. But these AA guys were saying, look, that's all right, but resentment and self-pity are really what does us in. It isn't just a matter of being a little paranoid. When you get resentment and self-pity, that's when you get drunk. Those are the two deadliest emotions we can have.

So we started telling alcoholics about all this in a lecture hall— hawking, spitting, skid row bums were learning what we knew about alcoholism. That became a major part of the program. They'd finish listening to the lecture, and afterward, instead of plotting how to get the next jug or how to escape, they'd start talking about the lecture and how wrong we were. It's not self-pity that does us in, they said; it's not that at all—it's my wife. And pretty soon they'd talk about all this and end up getting their heads shrunk from each other. Then some of the psychologists and social workers on the staff—we all knew different theoretical models—added some group therapy in with all this.

Finally, by 1953, Bradley and I got the Minnesota Civil Service Commission to hire recovering alcoholics to work on the staff with us. By the way, the professionals just thought that was crazy: why would you hire these drunks? They have no qualifications. But see, these alcoholics understood the phenomenon of addiction better than we did. They could ask questions that were more pointed than Bradley or I could, and they weren't afraid to ask them. They knew how to get at little things we didn't even know about, even though they didn't know how to do group psychotherapy. Instead of doing all this fancy theoretical stuff we were doing, the AAs learned to do what I call a task-oriented session. Here the group leader, who was recovering, said, look, my name is Tom Jones and I'm a recovering alcoholic. I've been sober about ten years now, and I've been working at Willmar for the last six months. And I'd just like to tell you people how it took me ten years before I could learn how to quit. What finally did it for me is realizing that I was a drunk, but it took me a long time to learn that. And until you learn that, you can't sober up. You have to learn what's wrong with you.

Then they'd go to the next person in the group: Joe, would you mind telling us why you're here at Willmar? Well, says Joe, my wife is going through menopause and I drink a little bit, and it's all blown out of proportion. And I don't know whether I'm an alcoholic or not, but I think I'd better stay here and listen. The next guy did something like this, and pretty soon they were all talking about their addiction.

All these sessions were task-oriented, focused on certain topics. So next time the leader said, look, today I want to tell you that what really helped me was finding out about resentment and self-pity. I used to be so resentful; I'd get so mad at people that I'd drink to kill myself to hurt them. And I finally realized that was crazy. Pretty soon the whole group would be be talking about that.

And they were relating to each other. They were relating as people who shared a common behavior, not common personalities. The addictive personality was superimposed on a bunch of heterogeneous people, but what they saw was their addictive personalities coming out: how they had been cheating, lying, and faking. The patients were facing up to some of this. So we found we could create a therapeutic environment.

The next crazy thing that happened in the early days at Willmar was unlocking the doors. We still had the alcoholics locked up, and the escape rate was anywhere from 22 to 37 percent. One night the alcoholics at Willmar were mad, and they wanted to talk to the superintendent. Bradley said, Dan, will you come in while I talk to them? And what the patients were doing was protesting: they didn't like being around mental patients, they didn't like eating with them—even though that was an improvement over what they were eating before! But you'd go over to the dining room and sit down, and the schizophrenic next to you would put his hand in your mashed potatoes. The food is better in the workhouse, said the alcoholics, and there's a better class of people there; we don't like all these crazy people. After all, we're not crazy. And we don't like it here. We don't like being locked up; we don't like this terrible place.

Bradley, in his characteristic way, said, okay, if you don't want to be here, go to hell. And he walked out. Two or three days later, he unlocked the doors. The escape rate dropped to 6 percent. So we learned—no hard science here, mind you—we learned that you don't need to lock alcoholics up.

By the way, our program was sixty days. And everybody back then knew you couldn't do anything in sixty days. That was too short. In those days, the wisdom was that you couldn't possibly help alcoholics unless you put them in a locked, secure psychiatric hospital for one to two years.

Now while all of this is happening at Willmar, something else is happening at Pioneer House and at Hazelden. It seems there's a kind of synchronicity. Is that really all it was, or was there a lot of back-and-forth exchange between these three programs?

We were working kind of independently, but the back-and-forth exchange happened. Pat Cronin was reading about AA in the Minneapolis Public Library. Two AA guys from Chicago came up to Minneapolis for the Little Brown Jug football game during the Armistice Day blizzard of 1941. The blizzard stranded them, so they dropped in and spent several days with Pat Cronin.

Pat sobered up, and the City of Minneapolis gave him permission to start Pioneer House. Social workers gave him permission, and judges, too. So he was picking up skid row bums in the Monday morning sentencing lineup, looking for the ones he thought he could help. Then Pat nodded to the judge, and the judge sent some to Pioneer House and the rest into jail. And at Pioneer House Pat was just doing a straight AA program.

Meanwhile, Hazelden started in 1949, also doing straight AA. These people thought they were going to improve on Pat Cronin's work. They were saying, Why do alcoholics have to wind up on skid row? Why not get them while they still have a job and family? It was a great idea. So Hazelden started, and nobody respectable came at first. The only people who came, through a grant from the Hill Foundation, were skid row bums. Even so, Hazelden was helping a lot of them. Then about 1952, Pat Butler sobered up, and in 1953 he started Fellowship Club, a halfway house to help homeless men. Hazelden was going broke, so Pat took over and kept it going. Pat then became a member of the legislative commission on alcoholism. He started going out to Willmar, visiting with Bradley and me, and we visited Pat at his home. We stole his literature on alcoholism, because we didn't have any money. He told us we could look in his library, but we just stole it, and he knew we were stealing it. Pat also gave me enough money to run away for eighteen months and get my

Ph.D. in 1956. He gave me enough money to go to the Yale Summer School of Alcohol Studies in 1954. He helped Bradley do some things, too.

By the way, Bradley wasn't a psychiatrist at that time, and I didn't even have a master's degree; I hadn't written the thesis yet. Bradley and I were doing this revolutionary stuff, and we had no formal qualifications; that was the crazy thing about it. But we were doing great things. And at the time it was just a terrible period of flux. Science was in a period of flux, and there were all kinds of competing explanations for addiction. And maybe there should be. By the way, those were the days when serotonin, the neurotransmitter, was first discovered. We knew serotonin was intimately related to schizophrenia and alcoholism, and we thought that both would be cured once they isolated serotonin.

Everybody thinks I should go around defending the Minnesota Model. But when Bradley and I developed it, it was a temporary thing. We never thought it would last. And the show has had too long a run, really. I say, I don't care what you replace it with; do anything that works. That's what we did in the first place. I mean, I have no sacred investment in the model.

The best wisdom I can see is AA. But even AA needs the reinforcement of good physical care, good detoxification. AA also needs somebody that understands mental illness enough to reduce some of those comorbidity problems found in some alcoholics. You need people who know enough about psychosocial forces, about how different people live and their value systems. And increasingly we're learning to be aware of incest and issues like that.

Clergy people need to be involved, too. They see real conversion experiences. You've got to be careful about what that word means: truly radical changes in lifestyles. As an alcoholic, I'm crazy, in a way. I might as well try this treatment thing out and see if it works. And then they see this radical change in their lives. The Minnesota Model works.

But it doesn't work for everybody, and that's the criticism. We're only helping 50 to 60 percent of the patients. Others are slipping, and we really don't know what the outcomes are, because the outcomes are never done quite scientifically enough. That's a criticism, and we are trying to improve our outcome studies.

But there's something about the whole thing that can't be reduced to science—the spirituality of the program. A few years ago I traveled to the former Soviet Union. At that time the Soviets would look at a recovering American—"My name is so-and-so and I've been in AA for ten years"—and say, nyet, nyet. You're no longer an alcoholic. They look down on alcoholics, hold them in contempt.

Then during one group meeting a Soviet woman in the audience, a physician, stood up and said: "I'm going to tell you that my husband is an alcoholic. He's been an alcoholic for ten years and I still love him." Then she sat down. That was a courageous thing for this woman to say. And an American, a recovering alcoholic, went over, sat down beside her, and put his arm around her. They both cried. Some of the Soviet people I was with said, "Now, I know what spirituality is." And it was a pretty damned good answer.

Endnotes

CHAPTER ONE:
BEFORE THE MINNESOTA MODEL

1. Alice Fleming, *Alcohol: The Delightful Poison—A History* (New York: Delacorte, 1975), 3.

2. Fleming, 4.

3. Fleming, 5.

4. Fleming, 8.

5. H. A. Guerber, *The Myths of Greece and Rome*, rev. Dorothy Margaret Stuart (New York: London House and Maxwell, 1938), 101-2.

6. Fleming, 15-16.

7. Mark Edward Lender and James Kirby Martin, *Drinking in America* (New York: Free Press, 1982), 32.

8. Fleming, 18.

9. Fleming, 8-9.

10. Fleming, 21.

11. Fleming, 19.

12. Fleming, 11.

13. Lender and Martin, 14.

14. Lender and Martin, 2.

15. Lender and Martin, 7.

16. Lender and Martin, 10.

17. Lender and Martin, 15-17.

18. Lender and Martin, 39.

19. Lender and Martin, 39.

20. Lender and Martin, 71.

21. Lender and Martin, 75.

22. Lender and Martin, 11.

23. Lender and Martin, 122-24.

24. Lender and Martin, 120-21.

25. Daniel J. Anderson, "A History of Our Confused Attitudes Toward Beverage Alcohol," *Mayo Clinic Proceedings* 42 (November 1967): 705-723.

26. Lender and Martin, 134.

27. Lender and Martin, 180.

28. *Alcoholics Anonymous* (New York: A.A. World Services, 1976), 24.

29. Ernest Kurtz, *Not-God: A History of Alcoholics Anonymous* (Center City, Minn.: Hazelden, 1979), 213.

30. *Alcoholics Anonymous Comes of Age* (New York: A.A. World Services, 1957), 63.

31. Kurtz, 29.

32. Mel B., *New Wine: The Spiritual Roots of the Twelve Step Miracle* (Center City, Minn.: Hazelden, 1991), 11.

33. Mel B., 13.

34. William James, *The Varieties of Religious Experience* (New York: New American Library, 1958), 297.

35. James, 298.

36. *Alcoholics Anonymous*, 569.

37. *Alcoholics Anonymous*, 44.

38. *Alcoholics Anonymous*, 47.

39. Ernest Kurtz, qtd. in Damian McElrath, *Hazelden: A Spiritual Odyssey* (Center City, Minn.: Hazelden, 1987), 44.

40. *44 Questions?* (New York: A.A. World Services, 1975), 7.

41. Mel B., 161.

42. Daniel J. Anderson, "Six Essentials of the Way," presentation handout, undated.

43. Anderson, "A History of Our Confused Attitudes," 4.

44. Fleming, 38-42.

45. Fleming, 43.

CHAPTER TWO:

THE MINNESOTA MODEL IS BORN — THREE CRUCIAL EXPERIMENTS

1. Daniel J. Anderson, *Perspectives on Treatment: The Minnesota Experience* (Center City, Minn.: Hazelden, 1981), 5.

2. Damian McElrath, *Hazelden: A Spiritual Odyssey* (Center City, Minn.: Hazelden, 1987), 47.

3. Interview with Glenn Farmer, undated.

4. Farmer interview.

5. Farmer interview.

6. Patrick J. Cronin, "The Twelve Steps of the Alcoholics Anonymous Program," transcribed presentations at Pioneer House, Minneapolis, Minn., undated.

7. Cronin, "The Twelve Steps."

8. Cronin, "The Twelve Steps."

9. McElrath, 39.

10. McElrath, 102.

11. McElrath, 44.

12. McElrath, 71.

13. McElrath, 70.

14. McElrath, 71.

15. Anderson, *Perspectives on Treatment*, 3.

16. Anderson, *Perspectives on Treatment*, 7.

17. Anderson, *Perspectives on Treatment*, 7-12

18. Anderson, *Perspectives on Treatment*, 12.

19. Anderson, *Perspectives on Treatment*, 13.

20. Anderson, *Perspectives on Treatment*, 14.

21. Anderson, *Perspectives on Treatment*, 16.

22. Anderson, *Perspectives on Treatment*, 18-19.

23. Anderson, *Perspectives on Treatment*, 20.

24. Anderson, *Perspectives on Treatment*, 21.

25. Anderson, *Perspectives on Treatment*, 23-24.

26. Anderson, *Perspectives on Treatment*, 18.

27. Anderson, *Perspectives on Treatment*, 17.

28. Anderson, *Perspectives on Treatment*, 26-27.

29. Anderson, *Perspectives on Treatment*, 27.

30. Anderson, *Perspectives on Treatment*, 30.

CHAPTER THREE:
UNDERSTANDING THE MINNESOTA MODEL

1. Kurtz, *Not-God*, 203.

2. Anderson, *Perspectives on Treatment*, 3.

3. Anderson, *Perspectives on Treatment*, 36.

4. Mark B. Sobell and Linda C. Sobell, *Behavioral Treatment of Alcohol Problems* (New York: Plenum, 1978).

5. E. Mansell Pattison, Mark B. Sobell, and Linda C. Sobell. *Emerging Concepts of Alcohol Dependence* (New York: Springer, 1977), 189-194.

6. J. Clark Laundergan, *Easy Does It: Alcoholism Treatment Outcomes, Hazelden and the Minnesota Model* (Center City, Minn.: Hazelden, 1982), 13.

7. Anderson, *Perspectives on Treatment*, 39.

8. Anderson, 40-51.

Chapter Four:
Progress and Problems—1950 to 1990

1. Daniel J. Anderson, "Celebrating 40 Years of Progress: A Look at the History of Alcohol/Drug Treatment" (Presentation to the 40th Annual Conference of the Alcohol and Drug Problems Association, August 1989).

2. Anderson, "Celebrating 40 Years of Progress."

3. Anderson, "Celebrating 40 Years of Progress."

4. Anderson, "Celebrating 40 Years of Progress."

5. Qtd. in Jellinek, E. M., *The Disease Concept of Alcoholism* (New Brunswick, N.J.: Hillhouse Press, 1960), 164.

6. Anderson, "Celebrating 40 Years of Progress."

7. Jellinek, 12.

8. Jellinek, 35.

9. Jellinek, 36.

10. Jellinek, 37.

11. Jellinek, 37.

12. Jellinek, 42-44.

13. Jellinek, 38.

14. Jellinek, 39.

15. Jellinek, 41-42.

16. Jellinek, 49-50.

17. Carlos Castaneda, *The Teachings of Don Juan: A Yacqui Way of Knowledge* (New York: Touchstone, 1968).

18. Anderson, "Celebrating 40 Years of Progress."

19. Anderson, "Celebrating 40 Years of Progress."

20. Anderson, "Celebrating 40 Years of Progress."

21. Anderson, "Celebrating 40 Years of Progress."

22. David J. Armor, J. Michael Polich, and Harriet B. Stambul, *Alcoholism and Treatment* (Santa Monica, CA: The Rand Corporation, 1976), 140.

23. Laundergan, 78-80.

24. Anderson, "Celebrating 40 Years of Progress."

25. Anderson, "Celebrating 40 Years of Progress."

26. Lender and Martin, 194.

27. Jeanne Engelmann, "America Ignores Its No. 1 Drug Problem—Alcohol," *Hazelden News and Professional Update*, May 1991.

28. "Hazelden Announces National Public Policy Campaign," *Hazelden News and Professional Update*, September 1991.

29. "Fiscal Therapy: Hazelden Struggles to Keep Care Center Profitable as Drug Admissions Decline," *Minneapolis Star Tribune*, 25 January 1993.

30. Engelmann.

31. Harold E. Hughes, "Recovering People Need to Join the Political Debate," *Hazelden News and Professional Update*, January 1992.

CHAPTER FIVE:
CRITICS AND CRITICISM

1. James Christopher, *Unhooked: Staying Sober and Drug-Free* (New York: Prometheus, 1989), 17.

2. Christopher, 21.

3. Christopher, 22-23.

4. Christopher, 47-48.

5. Christopher, 49-50.

6. Christopher, 51.

7. Jack Trimpey, *The Small Book* (New York: Delacorte, 1989), xxii.

8. Trimpey, xvii.

9. Trimpey, xxi.

10. Trimpey, xxi.

11. Trimpey, 102-5.

12. Jean Kirkpatrick, *Turnabout: New Help for the Woman Alcoholic* (New York: Bantam Books, 1977), 163.

13. Kirkpatrick, 160.

14. Kirkpatrick, 161.

15. Kirkpatrick, 162.

16. Herbert Fingarette, *Heavy Drinking: The Myth of Alcoholism as a Disease* (Berkeley: University of California, 1988), 3.

17. Fingarette, 21-22.

18. Fingarette, 38.

19. Fingarette, 52.

20. Fingarette, 56.

21. Fingarette, 57.

22. Fingarette, 65.

23. Fingarette, 24.

24. Fingarette, 25.

25. Fingarette, 27.

26. Fingarette, 73.

27. Fingarette, 99.

28. Stanton Peele, *The Diseasing of America: Addiction Treatment Out of Control* (Lexington, Mass: Lexington Books, 1989), 3.

29. Peele, 3.

30. Peele, 21.

31. Peele, 26-28.

32. Peele, viii.

33. Wendy Kaminer, *I'm Dysfunctional, You're Dysfunctional: The Recovery Movement and Other Self-Help Fashions* (Reading, Mass.: Addison Wesley, 1992), 71.

34. Kaminer, 83.

35. Kaminer, 28.

36. Kaminer, 70.

37. Kaminer, 164.

38. Kaminer, 21.

39. Kaminer, 6.

CHAPTER SIX:
THREE POINTS ABOUT THE MINNESOTA MODEL

1. Nan Robertson, *Getting Better: Inside Alcoholics Anonymous* (New York: William Morrow, 1988), 145.

2. Kurtz, 22.

3. George E. Vaillant, *The Natural History of Alcoholism: Causes, Common Patterns, and Paths to Recovery* (Cambridge, Mass.: Harvard University Press, 1983), 44.

4. Secretary of Health and Human Services, *Sixth Special Report to the U.S. Congress on Alcohol and Health* (U.S. Department of Health and Human Services, January 1987), 60.

5. Daniel J. Anderson, "Alcoholism Is Involuntary—Thus, a Disease," *Minneapolis Star Tribune*, 22 April 1989.

6. Laundergan, 15-16.

7. Jack H. Mendelson and Nancy K. Mello, *Alcohol: Its Use and Abuse in America* (Boston: Little Brown, 1985), 264.

8. Laundergan, 26.

9. Vaillant, 20.

10. Patricia Owen, "Chemical Dependency Research," in *Does Your Program Measure Up? An Addiction Professional's Guide for Evaluating Treatment Effectiveness*, by Jerry Spicer (Center City, Minn.: Hazelden 1991), 19-28.

11. Paul Higgins et al, "Treatment Outcomes for Minnesota Model Programs," in *Does Your Program Measure Up?* 102-111.

12. Norman G. Hoffman and Patricia Ann Harrison, "The Chemical Abuse Treatment Outcome Registry (CATOR): Treatment Outcome for Private Programs," in *Does Your Program Measure Up?* 121-122.

13. Laundergan, 138.

14. Laundergan, 144.

15. H. D. Holder, J. O. Blose, and M. J. Gasiorowski, *Alcoholism Treatment Impact on Total Health Care Utilization Costs: Analysis of the Federal Employee Health Benefit Program with Aetna Life Insurance Company* (Rockville, Md: NIAAA, 1985).

16. William R. Miller and Reid K. Hester, "Inpatient Alcoholism Treatment: Who Benefits?" *American Psychologist* 41 (July 1986): 794.

17. Miller and Hester, 802.

18. H. J. Harwood et al, *Economic Costs to Society of Alcohol and Drug Abuse and Mental Illness: 1980* (Research Triangle Park, N.C.: Research Triangle Institute, 1984).

19. Robertson, 221.

20. Peter Kizilos, "Hazelden Brings 12 Step Model to Corrections System," *Hazelden News and Professional Update*, May 1992.

Chapter Seven:
Challenges and Possible Futures

1. Anderson, "Chemical Dependency Futures" (Presentation to Institutional Advancement Staff, Hazelden Foundation, 17 May 1991).

2. Anderson, "The Minnesota Experience (1950-1960)," presentation handout, undated.

3. Anderson, *Perspectives on Treatment*, 54.

4. McElrath, 69.

Bibliography

Alcoholics Anonymous. New York: A.A. World Services, 1976.

Anderson, Daniel J. "A History of Our Confused Attitudes Toward Beverage Alcohol." *Mayo Clinic Proceedings* 42 (November 1967): 705-23.

Anderson, Daniel J. "Celebrating 40 Years of Progress: A Look at the History of Alcohol/Drug Treatment." Presentation to the 40th Annual Conference of the Alcohol and Drug Problems Association, August 1989.

Anderson, Daniel J. "Chemical Dependency Futures." Presentation to Institutional Advancement Staff, Hazelden Foundation, 17 May 1991.

Anderson, Daniel J. *Living with a Chronic Illness.* Center City, Minn.: Hazelden, 1986.

Anderson, Daniel J. *Perspectives on Treatment: The Minnesota Experience.* Center City, Minn: Hazelden, 1981.

Boche, H. Leonard. "The Minnesota Model: Will It Survive?" *C. D. Professional* (April-June 1991): 6-7.

Christopher, James. *Unhooked: Staying Sober and Drug-Free.* New York: Prometheus, 1989.

Cook, Christopher C. H. "The Minnesota Model in the Management of Drug and Alcohol Dependency: Miracle, Method or Myth? Part I. The Philosophy and the Programme." *British Journal of Addiction* 83 (June 1988): 625-34.

Cook, Christopher C. H. "The Minnesota Model in the Management of Drug and Alcohol Dependency: Miracle, Method or Myth? Part II. Evidence and Conclusions." *British Journal of Addiction* 83 (July 1988): 735-48.

Dorsman, Jerry. *How To Quit Drinking Without A. A.: A Complete Self-Help Guide.* Newark, Del.: New Dawn, 1991.

Douglas, Donald B. "Alcoholism as an Addiction: The Disease Concept Reconsidered." *Journal of Substance Abuse Treatment* 3 (1986): 115-20.

Fingarette, Herbert. *Heavy Drinking: The Myth of Alcoholism as a Disease.* Berkeley: University of California, 1988.

Fleming, Alice. *Alcohol: The Delightful Poison—A History.* New York: Delacorte Press, 1972.

44 Questions? New York: A.A. World Services, 1952.

Havens, Lisa M. "Understanding the Trends: A Guide to Cooperation Between Treatment Centers and Managed Care Providers." *Addiction & Recovery* (January/February 1991): 28-32.

Hill, Shirley Y. "The Disease Concept of Alcoholism: A Review." *Drug and Alcohol Dependence* 16 (1985): 193-214.

James, William. *The Varieties of Religious Experience.* New York: New American Library, 1958.

Jellinek, E. M. *The Disease Concept of Alcoholism.* New Brunswick, N.J.: Hillhouse Press, 1960.

Kaminer, Wendy. *I'm Dysfunctional, You're Dysfunctional: The Recovery Movement and Other Self-Help Fashions.* Reading, Mass.: Addison-Wesley, 1992.

Kirkpatrick, Jean. *Turnabout: New Help for the Woman Alcoholic.* New York: Bantam Books, 1977.

Kurtz, Ernest. *Not-God: A History of Alcoholics Anonymous.* Center City, Minn.: Hazelden, 1979.

Laundergan, J. Clark. *Easy Does It: Alcoholism Treatment Outcomes, Hazelden and the Minnesota Model.* Center City, Minn.: Hazelden, 1982.

Lender, Mark Edward, and James Kirby Martin. *Drinking in America.* New York: Free Press, 1982.

Madsen, William. *Defending the Disease of Alcoholism: From Facts to Fingarette.* Akron, Ohio: Wilson Brown, 1988.

McElrath, Damian. *Hazelden: A Spiritual Odyssey.* Center City, Minn.: Hazelden, 1987.

Mel B. *New Wine: The Spiritual Roots of the Twelve Step Miracle.* Center City, Minn.: Hazelden. 1991.

Mendelson, Jack H., and Nancy K. Mello. *Alcohol Use and Abuse in America.* Boston: Little Brown, 1985.

Miller, William R., and Reid K. Hester. "Inpatient Alcoholism Treatment: Who Benefits?" *American Psychologist* 41 (July 1986): 794-805.

Morse, Robert M. "Medicalizing the Minnesota Model." *Professional Counselor* (August 1991): 33-35.

Morse, Robert M., et al. "The Definition of Alcoholism." *Journal of the American Medical Association* 268 (26 August 1992): 1012-14.

Pattison, E. Mansell, Mark B. Sobell, and Linda C. Sobell. *Emerging Concepts of Alcohol Dependence.* New York: Springer, 1977.

Peele, Stanton. *The Diseasing of America: Addiction Treatment Out of Control.* Lexington, Mass: Lexington Books, 1989.

Richeson, Forrest. *"Courage to Change . . ."* Minneapolis: M&M, 1978.

Robertson, Nan. *Getting Better: Inside Alcoholics Anonymous.* New York: William Morrow, 1988.

Spicer, Jerry. "Quality Management and Clinical Pathways." *Strategies & Solutions: The Journal of Managed Mental Health Care* 1 (November 1992): 21-24.

Spicer, Jerry. *Does Your Program Measure Up? An Addiction Professional's Guide for Evaluating Treatment Effectiveness.* Center City, Minn.: Hazelden, 1991.

Tessina, Tina. *The Real Thirteenth Step: Discovering Confidence, Self Reliance, and Autonomy Beyond the Twelve Step Programs.* Los Angeles: J. P. Tarcher, 1991.

Trimpey, Jack. *The Small Book.* New York: Delacorte, 1989.

Vaillant, George E. *The Natural History of Alcoholism: Causes, Common Patterns, and Paths to Recovery.* Cambridge, Mass.: Harvard University Press, 1983.

Wallace, John. "Controlled Drinking, Treatment Effectiveness, and the Disease Model of Addiction: A Commentary on the Ideological Wishes of Stanton Peele." *Journal of Psychoactive Drugs* 22 (July-September 1990): 261-84.

Wesson, Donald R., David E. Smith, and Susan C. Steffens. *Crack and Ice: Treating Smokable Stimulant Abuse.* Center City, Minn.: Hazelden, 1992.

Index

ABOUT THE AUTHOR

Jerry Spicer became President and Chief Executive Officer of the
Hazelden Foundation in 1992. Prior to that he served as Senior Vice
President and Chief Operating Officer of the Foundation. He has
been associated with Hazelden since 1978, filling the various posts
of Vice President, Professional Services; Director of Employee Assistance, Research and Outreach; Assistant Director, Education and
Professional Services; and Manager of Evaluation and Applied Research. He is a member of the American College of Healthcare Ex-
ecutives and the American College of Addiction Treatment
Administrators. He holds master's degrees in sociology and hospital
administration. His special interests are in research, health care administration, and writing. He has been the author of twenty articles
and four books, including *The EAP Solution* and *Does Your Program
Measure Up?*

Other titles that will interest you . . .

Does Your Program Measure Up?
An Addiction Professional's Guide for Evaluating Treatment Effectiveness
by Jerry Spicer, M.H.A.

To effectively contain costs and maintain quality service, you need to be able to evaluate your program's achievements. This book provides you with methods to measure, record, analyze, and institute changes to bring added success to your addiction treatment program—from admittance to aftercare. And it discusses program evaluation, future trends, and relevant case studies. 240 pp.
Order No. 5057

The EAP Solution
Current Trends and Future Issues
edited by Jerry Spicer, M.H.A.

This comprehensive guide to employee assistance programs provides you with vital information about current models, issues, options, and future trends. Editor Jerry Spicer—together with sixteen other authors—provides an overview of the complex field of EAPs. This book also encourages you to develop new alternatives to meet the needs of a complex and diverse clientele. 219 pp.
Order No. 5095

Dual Disorders
Counseling Clients with Chemical Dependency and Mental Illness
Second Edition
by Dennis C. Daley, M.S.W., Howard Moss, M.D.,
and Frances Campbell, R.N., M.S.N., C.S.

This book is a practical, must-read resource for mental health and chemical dependency counselors. The focus here is on educational, cognitive, and behavioral interventions you can use in your daily work with clients with dual disorders and their families. 140 pp.
Order No. 5023
